PUBLICATIONS OF THE FACULTY OF ARTS
OF THE UNIVERSITY OF MANCHESTER

No. 16

ANGEL GANIVET'S
IDEARIUM ESPAÑOL

A CRITICAL STUDY

ANGEL GANIVET'S
IDEARIUM ESPAÑOL

A CRITICAL STUDY

by

H. RAMSDEN

*Professor of Spanish Language and Literature
in the University of Manchester*

MANCHESTER
UNIVERSITY PRESS

© 1967
Published by the University of Manchester at
THE UNIVERSITY PRESS
316–324 Oxford Road, Manchester 13

SBN: 7190 1240 6

Printed in Great Britain by Butler & Tanner Ltd, Frome and London

CONTENTS

I quote some of the headings of the seventeen extracts from reviews: 'Amazing and monumental. . . . An immortal masterpiece. . . . The greatest work of our time. . . . A literary and intellectual phenomenon. . . . Probably the greatest historical work ever written. . . . A landmark, perhaps even a turning point.' This chorus of praise is a chastening reminder of the very restricted influence exercised by [serious] criticism. The effect it had on me was nevertheless a heartening one. I have sometimes felt the uncomfortable thought stirring: 'Is it still worth while?' Apparently it *is* still worth while. For we must never abdicate before misdirected popular enthusiasm.

Pieter Geyl, *Debates with Historians*,
London 1955, p. 178.

I

ANGEL GANIVET: LIFE, WORKS AND FAME

THE BASIC CHRONOLOGY: LIFE AND WORKS[1]

Granada, 1865–88

Angel Ganivet was born in Granada on 13 December 1865, the second of six children. His father, the owner of a modest flour mill, died in 1875, and at twelve the boy left school and worked for a time in a solicitor's office before going on, at fourteen, to the local grammar school and thence, at nineteen, to the University of Granada where he studied simultaneously Law and Arts. Intelligence and hard work; the avoidance of student revels;

---

[1] Except where otherwise stated, references in this study are to the Aguilar two-volume edition of Ganivet's *Obras completas* (3rd ed., Madrid 1961–2). A simple page number indicates that the reference is to *Idearium español* (I, 147–305); references to other works give also the volume number. Italics in quotations are Ganivet's unless I declare them to be mine. Where I have preferred the reading of a first edition I have used it [in brackets].

Because of continuing doubts and errors on the subject, I shall indicate, in this first section, the chronology of composition of Ganivet's various works and the dates of first publication: in article form, where applicable, and in book form. If the reader finds these pages irrelevant to my main theme it is hoped he will also find them useful. In all cases I have seen the publications myself, but my perusal of *El Defensor de Granada* would have been more laborious—and doubtless less successful—if I had lacked the invaluable guidance of Luis Seco de Lucena Paredes' bibliography (in *Juicio de Angel Ganivet sobre su obra literaria*, Granada 1962, pp. 156–60). In describing first book-editions, I take my information from the title page and add supplementary information, usually from the wrappers, between square brackets. In each case I indicate also the number of significant pages whether numbered or not (i.e. including indices and errata lists, but excluding advertisements and end leaves).

For other references and abbreviations, see below, p. 196.

distinctions and prizes—this, it appears, is the story of
Angel Ganivet's life during the years 1880–8. In 1888 he
completed his Arts degree and moved to Madrid in order
to pursue post-graduate and professional studies.

Madrid, 1888–92

Apart from a liaison, from 1891, with a certain Amelia
Roldán, who was to form an intermittent part of his
household during the next seven years and to bear him
two children, Ganivet appears to have allowed himself
little distraction from his studies: during 1888–9 he prepared his doctorate examinations and wrote two theses;[1] in
1889 he qualified as a Government archivist and thereby
assured his position in the capital; in 1890 he completed
his Granada Law degree; in 1891 he worked for a University Chair of Greek but was unsuccessful. Finally, in May
1892 he came first in the examinations for the Spanish
Consular Service and was appointed Spanish vice-consul
in Antwerp.[2]

Antwerp, 1892–6

Ganivet took up his appointment in July 1892. Unsociable
by nature and separated now from his few enthusiastic

---

[1] *España filosófica contemporánea* (II, 577–662) and *Importancia de la
lengua sánscrita* (I, 865–939). The first was unsuccessful; the second was
read and approved on 28 October 1889. Ganivet was subsequently
awarded the *premio extraordinario* for an essay entitled 'Doctrinas varias
de los filósofos sobre el concepto de causa y verdadero origen y sub-
jetivo valor de este concepto' (31 January 1890; I, 941–53).

España filosófica contemporánea was first published in ANGEL GANIVET,
Obras completas, IX (Francisco Beltrán and Victoriano Suárez, Madrid
1930), pp. 7–100. *Importancia de la lengua sánscrita* and 'Doctrinas varias...'
were published in MP, 1920, pp. 3–118, 119–36.

[2] Also during these years in Madrid, it appears, Ganivet wrote his essay
'El mundo soy yo o el hombre de las dos caras' (first published by Hans
Jeschke in *La Gaceta Literaria*, 15 November 1928; not in *OC*, but in
Javier Herrero, *Angel Ganivet: un iluminado*, Madrid 1966, pp. 284–90).

Spanish friends, he seems to have spent much of his time in Antwerp in a realm of ideas, reading extensively, observing life rather than living it and intellectualizing his impressions. 'Recogido dentro de mí mismo, por falta de medios de comunicación,' he writes, 'todas las fuerzas se gastan en cavilar y barajar ideas y planes' (II, 907). Many of these ideas and plans are revealed in letters to his friend Francisco Navarro Ledesma (18 February 1893 to 4 January 1895; II, 809–1017) and these are an invaluable source of information on Ganivet's thought and personality during his first years of residence abroad.[1] Moreover, the *Epistolario* throws light on the genesis of Ganivet's first important literary work, *La conquista del reino de Maya por el último conquistador español Pío Cid* (I, 307–657), most of which was apparently written from June to October 1893.[2] Finally, also written during Ganivet's three and a

[1] ANGEL GANIVET | *Epistolario* | (publisher's device) | Madrid | Biblioteca Nacional y Extranjera | Leonardo Williams, Editor | Lista, núm. 8 | 1904   (292 pp.)
['Prólogo' by F. Navarro y Ledesma, pp. 7–31; Ganivet's *Epistolario*, pp. 33–287; 'Indice', pp. 289–92]
According to Navarro these thirty-one letters represent only about a tenth of those that Ganivet actually wrote to him (op. cit., p. 9). In *Helios* I–IV (1903–4) he published fourteen letters from Ganivet (31 August 1891 to 25 April 1896), ten of them not included in the above *Epistolario* or in the *Obras completas*. They have recently been republished in Herrero, op. cit., pp. 291–331.
The following also are important collections of Ganivet's correspondence:
    (1) NML, pp. 41–117 (24 letters to Nicolás María López, 25 May 1895 to 10 November 1898).
    (2) LSLP, pp. 83–114 (17 letters to Luis or Francisco Seco de Lucena, [October/November 1895] to 11 November 1898).
    (3) [to appear shortly] *Angel Ganivet: Correspondencia familiar, 1888–1897.* Ed. Javier Herrero, Editorial Anel, Granada.
None of this correspondence is included in the *Obras completas*.
[2] The years of Ganivet's stay in Antwerp were years of European colonization in Africa, and Belgium was taking an active part. In May 1893 Ganivet wrote of the venture with distaste and reported the death from yellow fever of a Nicaraguan just back from the Congo (II, 819–21;

4 IDEARIUM ESPAÑOL

half years as Spanish vice-consul in Antwerp, are four
articles: one from the beginning of his stay and three from
the end.[1]

Helsingfors, 1896–8

At the end of 1895 Ganivet was promoted to consul and
1896 in January 1896 he moved to his new post: in Helsingfors

cf. *Idearium*, 252–6). A month later we find him immersed in African
travel books, 'que es el continente que me simpatiza más' (II, 838), and
referring to his 'planes científicos y literarios, de los cuales algún día te
hablaré' (II, 842). A week later, still in June, he writes again about his
reading of travel literature and expresses his preference for writings by
resident Europeans who understand the language and the life of the
natives (II, 855). On 24 July Ganivet reports that he is completely
free from consular duties and that he is up to Chapter 11 of a work
that he hopes to publish on his return to Spain (II, 879); on 18 August
he has completed seventeen chapters and expects the work to have
twenty-three (II, 882); a month later he reports that the work is almost
ready and it becomes clear from his description that it is in fact *La
conquista del reino de Maya* (II, 903–6). In October he has still not finished
writing, but he is anxious to get the book off his mind before passing to
'otras cosas de más jugo' (II, 913). The last page of the manuscript bears
the date 'Diciembre 1893' (photograph in Joaquín de Entrambasaguas,
Las mejores novelas contemporáneas, I, Barcelona 1957, 1125), but almost
two years later Ganivet apparently took up his manuscript again for re-
vision, for on 11 October 1895 he announced to his sisters: 'Quizás esta
noche acabe el libro' (AGM, p. 106). The manuscript ('un libro . . . que
está acabado desde 1893') was still not in the hands of the printer on
6 May 1896, 'por mi horror innato a las letras de molde' (NML, p. 65),
nor, apparently, on 29 August 1896 (NML, p. 71). On 3 February 1897,
however, Ganivet was busy proof-correcting and he refers to the work
as 'ya casi impreso' (NML, p. 76). It finally appeared in April 1897
(NML, pp. 76–8; notice in *La Revista Moderna*, 10 April):
    La conquista | *del* | *reino de Maya* | *por el último conquistador español* | *Pío
Cid* | compuesto por | ANGEL GANIVET | Madrid | Est. Tip. "Sucesores
de Rivadeneyra" | 1897   (385 pp.)
[1] 'Un festival literario en Amberes' (*DG*, 21 August 1892; not in *OC*);
'Lecturas extranjeras' (*DG*, 4 October 1895; I, 967–73); 'Arte gótico'
(*DG*, 17 November 1895; I, 985–93); 'Socialismo y música' (*DG*, 23
November 1895; I, 975–84).
The first of these articles has apparently not been published in book
form. 'Arte gótico' and 'Socialismo y música' were reproduced in
ANGEL GANIVET, *Hombres del Norte y artículos varios*, Granada 1905
(pp. 79–88, 89–100) and 'Lecturas extranjeras' in MP, 1918 (pp. 27–35;
with the republication of the previous two articles, pp. 51–62, 37–50).

(now Helsinki) in the Russian Grand Duchy of Finland. For some time he had been reading works on urban aesthetics and considering the solutions proposed for the various foreign towns known to him. Now, in his journey from Antwerp to Helsingfors, his contact with further foreign cities (Berlin, Königsberg and St. Petersburg) prompted reflections on his own native Granada, 'vista a distancia y comparada con otras ciudades' (LSLP, p. 87). The result was a series of twelve articles written during the first weeks of his arrival in the Finnish capital (14 to 27 February 1896) and published in *El Defensor de Granada* under the general title *Granada la bella* (29 February to 13 April 1896; I, 57–145).[1]

But already, it appears, Ganivet was working also on his most celebrated work, *Idearium español*, for in the sixth article of *Granada la bella* we read:

> Para entretener mis ocios estoy escribiendo un libro que trata de algo parecido a esto de que ahora hablo: de la constitución ideal de la raza española (I, 100).

But how much of the *Idearium* had Ganivet written in February 1896? We do not know. Nor do we know whether, after completing *Granada la bella*, he was able to return to the *Idearium* before the spring thaw reopened the port of Helsingfors to shipping and brought with it the increase that Ganivet had anticipated in his consular duties (LSLP, p. 86). What we do know is that on 6 May Ganivet wrote

---

[1] The twelve articles were subsequently published privately in book form and appeared in August 1896 (LSLP, p. 91; notice in *Apuntes*, 6 September 1896):

Granada | la | bella | Edición privada| Helsingfors | [J. C. Frenckell & Sons Boktryckeri] | 1896   (94 pp.)

[The identity of the author is indicated only by the *dedicatoria* (cf. *OC* I, 59)]

to Nicolás María López informing him that he had 'un cajón lleno de poesías [. . .] escri[tas] en francés directamente la mayor parte' (NML, p. 63) and it appears that these poems had been written since his arrival in Helsingfors three months earlier (AGM. p. 133).[1] We know, too, that in June 1896 Ganivet wrote another article for *El Defensor de Granada*,[2] and that on 19 August he was planning to stay in Helsingfors until March and was looking forward to the approaching winter so that he could devote himself to a series of 'Cartas de Finlandia' (LSLP, pp. 91–92). But his immediate energies, it appears, were devoted to the *Idearium* and on 29 August he wrote to Nicolás María López:

> hoy me encuentro en un estado de postración espiritual que a ti mismo te daría lástima, y ahora es cuando trabajo más, sin saber cómo, sin hacerme cargo, ni tener idea de lo que me sale; no sé si es bueno o malo; pero sospecho que es mejor de lo que antes hacía, y me dejaba la impresión de algo discreto. Es decir, que ahora podré cometer majaderías estupendas, sin estar en mi mano enmendarlas ni conocerlas; pero quizás me salga algo que las compense. Estoy componiendo un libro pequeño (pues no me gustan los grandes), una ideología que desde luego te aseguro es mejor que lo que hace . . .,[3] que dicho sea de paso, acude demasiado a lo *nuevo* para abrirse camino, y que quizá luego nos resulte una especie de Schopenhauer, vestido de corte (NML, pp. 69–70).

[1] These poems are not in *OC*. A selection has been published by Juan del Rosal in *Angel Ganivet, semblanza, traducción y selección*, Colección 'Poetas españoles', Barcelona 1940. See also AGM, pp. 131–6, and MFA, 'La poesía de Ganivet', in *Insula* 228–9, November–December 1965.

[2] 'La pintura española juzgada en el extranjero' (*DG*, 10 July 1896; I, 995–1003). The article was first republished in MP, 1918 (pp. 75–85).

[3] The name omitted by Nicolás María López was that of Miguel de Unamuno (AGM, p. 127).

At the end of August, then, the *Idearium* was well advanced and Ganivet was still working on it. The date at the end of the text, 'Octubre 1896', presumably indicates the month of completion.[1]

But Ganivet cannot have devoted much time to the *Idearium* in October, for on the first day of that month he completed the first of his *Cartas finlandesas* and by the end of the month he had written six more (LSLP, pp. 157–8). Thereafter, progress was slower and the twentieth letter was not completed until the following spring (after 9 *1897* March 1897 but probably before the end of the month).[2] But by then the thaw was bringing with it an increase in consular duties. On 20 April Ganivet informed Nicolás María López that he had applied for four months' leave and, on 15 May, that his application had been granted (NML, pp. 77, 79). He handed over his responsibilities to the honorary vice-consul and set out for Spain on 1 June (AGM, p. 137). He was to return towards the end of September—in time for the winter months of consular inactivity.

Ganivet spent the summer of 1897 in Spain, principally

[1] The book appeared in August 1897 (notice in *La Revista Moderna*, 14 August 1897; see also LSLP, p. 94):
   [ÁNGEL GANIVET] | *Idearium | español* | Granada | [Tip. Lit. Vda. e Hijos de Sabatel, Mesones, 52] | 1897   (164 pp.)
[2] There was then a break of twelve months before the two final letters were written: in the spring of 1898, when the series was being prepared for publication in book form.
   The first twenty letters were published in *El Defensor de Granada* from 14 October 1896 to 9 July 1897, letters 21 and 22, also in *El Defensor*, on 20 and 26 April 1898. The twenty-two letters (I, 659–864) appeared in book form in September 1898 (LSLP, p. 107; notice in *La Alhambra*, 30 September 1898):
   Cartas finlandesas | de | ÁNGEL GANIVET | Cónsul de España en Helsingfors | Granada | Tip. Lit. Vda. e Hijos de Sabatel, Mesones, 52 | 1898   (liv + 212 pp.)
   [Nicolás María López, 'Ganivet y sus obras', pp. v–liv; *Cartas finlandesas*, pp. 1–209; 'Indice', pp. 211–12]

in Granada where he became the driving force behind the
local literary and artistic group, the *Cofradía del Avellano*,
was honoured with a banquet, and stimulated members
of the group to collaborate with him in a book of homage
to their native city, to be published under the title *Libro de
Granada*. Contributions were allocated and, almost immediately, Ganivet wrote four of the eight for which he
was to be responsible.[1] From Sitges (Catalonia), where he
spent a month's holiday with his family (mid August to
mid September) he announced that he had completed
three more (NML, p. 81) and on the same day, 4 September, he sent his friend Francisco Seco de Lucena an article
on the Catalan artistic group, Cau Ferrat (LSLP, p. 94).[2]

Back in Helsingfors, towards the end of September,
Ganivet informed Seco de Lucena that he had now completed his contributions to the *Libro de Granada* (LSLP,
p. 99),[3] and he outlined his plans for the immediate future:

Una vez que me vea libre de trabajos oficinescos pienso
dedicarme a escribir los artículos que aparecerán bajo el
título de *Hombres del Norte*. Los primeros serán sobre los
noruegos Jonas Lie, Ibsen, Björ[n]son, Garborg, Kielland,

[1] Published, together with contributions by other collaborators, in
DG, 7, 13, 21, 27 July 1897; see below for republication in book form;
II, 685–702.
[2] *DG*, 12 September 1897; republished in *Hombres del Norte y artículos
varios*, Granada 1905 (pp. 118–26); II, 725–30.
[3] Of these last four contributions, 'Un bautizo' (II, 713–19) was published in *La Alhambra* (30 November 1898). The other three (II, 665–83,
703–11, 721–4) seem not to have appeared until *Libro de Granada* itself
was published, in April 1899 (see *La Alhambra*, 31 March 1899), delayed
by the lesser dynamism of some of Ganivet's fellow contributors:
  Libro de Granada | Texto | de | ANGEL GANIVET—GABRIEL RUIZ DE
ALMODÓVAR | MATÍAS MÉNDEZ VELLIDO—NICOLÁS MARÍA LÓPEZ |
Ilustraciones | de | ADOLFO LOZANO—ISIDORO MARÍN | JOSÉ RUIZ DE
ALMODÓVAR | RAFAEL LATORRE | Granada | Imp. Lit. Vda. e Hijos
de P. V. Sabatel, | Mesones, núm. 52 | 1899.   (216 pp.

Hamsun, los Krag, etc. etc. Como esto exige mucha lectura, irán dos al mes y empezaremos en noviembre (LSLP, p. 97).

But if Ganivet started work on these articles he did not work on them for long, for on 1 December 1897 he began to write his second novel, *Los trabajos del infatigable creador Pío Cid* (NML, p. 90), and during the immediately follow- *1898* ing months this occupied most of his energies.[1] On 18 March 1898 he informed Luis Seco de Lucena that he was very busy finishing the novel and that the first part (two volumes) was at press (LSLP, p. 103). 'En cuanto termine esta faena,' he continued, 'apretaré más en los *Hombres del Norte.*'

But *Hombres del Norte* had not been completely neglected during the writing of *Los trabajos*. On 26 January 1898 Ganivet had sent Francisco Seco de Lucena 'la primera

[1] Ganivet had had this work in mind for some time, and on 15 May 1897, in commenting on *La conquista del reino de Maya*, he had looked forward to publishing, 'si llega el día, los trabajos de Pío Cid en España' (NML, p. 80). But until 1 December 1897 he apparently wrote nothing. Thereafter, on 29 December, he announced: 'Voy por la cuartilla 114, unas 150 de impresión. Ahora no trajabo más que en esto, y voy a ver si en dos meses más puedo rematarlo' (NML, p. 88). He completed the intended first volume (five *trabajos*) on 31 January 1898 and immediately sent it off to press, estimating that it would give 400 pages (NML, p. 90). Subsequently, two of these five *trabajos* were held over for the second volume, with the addition of one more *trabajo* (NML, p. 92). On 18 March Ganivet announced that both volumes were at press and were expected to appear by May (LSLP, p. 103). The first volume was in fact despatched to friends in May 1898 (NML, p. 97) and was mentioned in *La Alhambra* on 30 June 1898. However, it was not put on sale until 12 October 1898, when the second volume was ready (LSLP, p. 111; see also NML, pp. 97, 105, 110, 116; LSLP, p. 106):
  Los trabajos | del infatigable creador | Pío Cid | compuestos por | ANGEL GANIVET | Tomo I/Tomo II | Madrid | Est. Tip. "Sucesores de Rivadeneyra" | 1898 (287 + 323 pp.)
These two volumes, then, cover Pío Cid's first six 'labours' (II, 7–575); the remaining six were still unwritten when Ganivet died. Part of the fifth labour, 'Juanico el ciego' (II, 405–24), was serialized in *La Alhambra*, Nos. 7–10 (15, 30 April, 15, 31 May 1898).

muestra' ('Jonas Lie'), a few weeks later the second
('Bjornstjerne Bjornson') and a few weeks later still—in
mid March—the third ('Arne Garborg').[1] In March also
Ganivet wrote the final chapters of *Cartas finlandesas* and
sent the work to press (see above, p. 7, n. 2; LSLP, pp. 38,
98-9, 102-4), and during the following months he completed three further articles in the series *Hombres del Norte*
('Henrik Ibsen', 'Vilhelm Krag', 'Knut Hamsun')[2] and,
amidst 'viajes y arreglos oficinescos', wrote 'a vuela pluma'
his own contribution to a public exchange of letters with
Miguel de Unamuno on the future of Spain (LSLP, p.
105).[3]

[1] LSLP, pp. 99, 103, 159.
[2] The six articles of *Hombres del Norte* appeared as follows:
'Jonas Lie' (*DG*, 4 February 1898; II, 1021-31)
'Bjornstjerne Bjornson' (*DG*, 2 March 1898; II, 1031-41)
'Arne Garborg' (*DG*, 27 March 1898; not in *OC*, but in LSLP, pp. 125-33)
'Henrik Ibsen' (*DG*, 22-3 June 1898; II, 1042-56)
'Vilhelm Krag' (*DG*, 27 August 1898; not in *OC*, but in LSLP, pp. 133-9)
'Knut Hamsun' (*DG*, 30 August 1898; not in *OC*, but in LSLP, pp.
139-44)
They were not published in book form until 1905:
    Hombres del Norte | y | artículos varios | por | ANGEL GANIVET | con
un prólogo de | Rafael Gago Palomo | Granada | Imprenta de El
Defensor de Granada | 1905.   (viii + 127 pp.)
[*Hombres del Norte*, pp. 5-76. The 'artículos varios', pp. 77-126, are
'Arte gótico', 'Socialismo y música', 'Trogloditas', 'El alma de las
calles' and 'Cau Ferrat'. The article 'Knut Hamsun', pp. 69-76, is
omitted from the List of Contents, p. 127]
On 31 October 1898 Ganivet wrote to Francisco Seco de Lucena:
    En cuanto me quede algún respiro te enviaré dos *Hombres del Norte*
que tengo empezados a hilvanar: Jacobsen y Brandés, y en diciembre
espero escribir otros dos: Rydberg y Heidenstam, y así sucesivamente
(LSLP, pp. 109-10).
These articles were apparently not written.
[3] *El porvenir de España* (pub. *DG*). Ganivet's contribution appeared
from 9 to 15 July 1898 (in five parts; II, 1059-79) and from 6 to 14 September 1898 (in four parts, II, 1080-95). His July contribution, but not
his September contribution, was published in book form in 1905:
    Angel T. de Ganivet—Editor | Hombres del Norte | El porvenir de
España | por | ANGEL GANIVET | Madrid | Librería General de Vic-
toriano Suárez | 48, Preciados, 48 | 1905   (111 pp.)
[*El porvenir de España*, pp. 71-111. The section *Hombres del Norte*,

Riga, *August to November 1898*

The journeys referred to in Ganivet's letter to Francisco
Seco de Lucena were occasioned by his imminent transfer
to the Spanish consulate in Riga (Russia), and it was from
there that he sent the second part of his contribution to
El porvenir de España (LSLP, p. 106). Letters written by
him during his first weeks in Riga show him keen to continue and to extend the range of his *Hombres del Norte*
(LSLP, pp. 104, 106). But his next article, it appears, was
'Nuestro espíritu misterioso',[1] and during the following
weeks he sent off two articles for inclusion in the Madrid
periodical *Vida Nueva.*[2] In October we find him writing
a play, *El escultor de su alma*, and referring to the problems
of production in 'Una idea', an article dedicated to his
friends in Granada for their kindness in publishing *Cartas
finlandesas* in book form.[3] The play itself was sent off to

pp. 5-69, includes only the articles on Lie, Bjornson and Ibsen]
The first complete book edition of the exchange (both writers):
    MIGUEL DE UNAMUNO | y | ANGEL GANIVET | *El porvenir* | *de España*
| (publisher's   device) | Madrid | Renacimiento | Sociedad   Anónima
Editorial | Pontejos, 3. | 1912   (170 pp.)
    [Publisher's Introduction, pp. 7-8; Unamuno's 'Aclaraciones previas',
pp. 9-20; text of the exchange, pp. 21-170]
The most easily accessible complete text of the exchange (together with
Unamuno's 'Aclaraciones previas') is the following:
    MIGUEL DE UNAMUNO, *Obras completas*, IV (Afrodisio Aguado,
Barcelona 1958), 951-1015.
[1] *DG*, 16 September 1898; not in *OC*; apparently first republished in
LSLP, pp. 148-53.
[2] '¡Naññ̃! . . .' was published in *Vida Nueva* on 16 October 1898;
'Mis inventos', received in Madrid a few days before the author's death,
appeared posthumously in the same periodical on 1 January 1899, 'primero
de una serie que iba a escribir expresamente para nuestro periódico' (loc.
cit.). To the best of my knowledge neither has been published in book
form.
[3] *DG* 26 October 1898; not in *OC*; apparently first republished in
LSLP, pp. 145-8.
Also to this period belongs 'España y Rusia (Nuevos horizontes
comerciales)', a consular report dated 4 October 1898 (first published in
MP, 1920, pp. 139-54; I, 955-65).

B

Francisco Seco de Lucena on 11 November 1898,[1] with
the promise of two further *Hombres del Norte* articles for
the following week. They did not arrive. On 29 November 1898, after weeks of agitation and extreme depression,
Ganivet committed suicide by throwing himself into the
River Dvina. Mere days before, a local doctor had diag-
nosed a dangerous state of general progressive paralysis
and persecution mania and recommended immediate con-
finement to an asylum.[2] Many other factors have been
suggested as having contributed to Ganivet's suicide: his
isolation from friends, his vegetarianism, the rigours of a
northern climate, constant overwork, his lack of religious
faith, a family history of insanity, Spanish misfortunes in
Cuba, the imminent arrival in Riga of Amelia Roldán
(because Ganivet was afraid he might be persuaded to
forgive her for her alleged infidelity, say some commentators; because he was ashamed to have her see him in his
distressed condition, says another). . . .

GANIVET'S FAME

The first signs of recognition

Ganivet vivió obscurecido. Su fama apenas traspasó el
estrecho círculo local de la ciudad en que había nacido y el

---

[1] II, 731–808. The play was first produced in Granada in the theatre
Isabel la Católica on 1 March 1899. It was not published until 1904:

El escul+tor de su alma | Drama místico | compuesto por | ÁNGEL
GANIVET | precedido de un prólogo por | Francisco Seco de Lucena |
Granada | Imprenta de El Defensor de Granada. | 1904　　(115 pp.)

[Francisco Seco de Lucena, 'Algo acerca de Ganivet', pp. 3–35; Ganivet's manuscript title page, p. 37; 'Personajes', p. 38; 'Indicaciones para
la representación', p. 39; Text, pp. 41–112; Editorial Note, p 113;
'Fé de Erratas', p. 115]

[2] On the circumstances of Ganivet's death, see especially Enrique
Domínguez Rodiño, 'En los umbrales de Rusia', in *El Imparcial,* 9 December 1920, 14, 21, 23 January 1921.

no más amplio de sus amistades particulares. Sólo muy al
final de su vida empezaron a ser apreciadas sus obras. Su
verdadera celebridad ha sido póstuma (E. Gómez de Baquero, in *La España Moderna*, August 1904, p. 171).

Of course, it could hardly have been otherwise. Apart
from a still little known article published in August 1892
and three slight articles that appeared in October-Novem-
ber 1895—all of them in a provincial paper of little
national significance—Ganivet published nothing until
after his thirtieth birthday, and he died before he was
thirty-three. Moreover, even after his thirtieth year, he
confined his periodical collaboration almost exclusively to
the same provincial paper and did not publish his first
book, *Granada la bella*, a limited private edition 'para dentro de casa' (LSLP, p. 91), until August 1896. Only with
the publication of *La conquista del reino de Maya* (in April
1897) and that of *Idearium español* (in August 1897) did
Ganivet seek to attract attention outside his native
city.

But outside Granada, it appears, he did not find the
immediate, open-hearted acclaim that his friends were
bestowing upon him in his native city, and in the prologue to the 1898 edition of *Cartas finlandesas*—one of the
most balanced and most searching of early studies on
Ganivet's writings—his friend Nicolás María López declared:

> El *Idearium*, a pesar de su importancia, pasó desapercibido;
> nadie (que yo sepa) dijo una palabra de él; fuera de Granada,
> la prensa de Madrid [. . .] no se fijó siquiera en este libro de
> tan jugosa labor intelectual (op. cit., p. xxi).

In fact, the neglect was rather less than these lines suggest
and Francisco Navarro Ledesma, a well-known writer

and an intimate friend of Ganivet in Madrid, had long
since drawn attention to the *Idearium* as 'un libro de raro
mérito, de admirable profundidad y que merece ser leída
atentamente'.[1] Moreover, immediately after the appearance of the *Idearium*, the Barcelona daily *La Vanguardia*
had reproduced the final pages of the book (295–305)
and presented the author as 'uno de los jóvenes que con
Rafael Altamira y otros [. . .] honran a la generación que
está ahora llegando a la plenitud' (11 September 1897).
Ganivet himself, then on holiday in Catalonia, was able to
report to his friend Francisco Seco de Lucena that the
book was selling well there and being discussed (albeit
with some distaste on the part of *catalanistas*), and that
the editor of *La Vanguardia* had visited him in Sitges to
invite his collaboration in the paper (12 September 1897;
LSLP, pp. 96–8).[2] Moreover, even as Nicolás María
López was writing his prologue (July 1898), Leopoldo
Palacios, a critic who knew Ganivet only from his publications, was likewise lamenting the unjust neglect of
Ganivet's works and preparing a long and enthusiastic
review of *La conquista del reino de Maya* and *Idearium
español* for inclusion in the June-September fascicle of
Rafael Altamira's *Revista Crítica de Historia y Literatura*
(III, 1898, 274–80), to be followed in the next fascicle

[1] In the Madrid weekly, *La Revista Moderna* (14 August 1897). See
also Navarro Ledesma's enthusiastic references to *Granada la bella* (in
Apuntes, 6 September 1896) and to *La conquista del reino de Maya* (in
La Revista Moderna, 10 April 1897). Also in Madrid, *Granada la bella* had
attracted the attention of at least two other notable critics: Jacinto
Octavio Picón (in *El Imparcial*, 5 October 1896) and Mariano de Cavia
('hace dos años ya,' wrote Rodrigo Soriano in *Los Lunes de El Imparcial*,
5 December 1898, but I have been unable to trace Cavia's article).
[2] The only subsequent contribution of Ganivet to *La Vanguardia* that
I have been able to trace is Letter 9 of his *Cartas finlandesas*, published on
8 October 1897 under the title 'Estética femenina'. It had appeared nine
months earlier in *El Defensor de Granada*.

by a review of *Los trabajos* by Altamira himself (III, 1898, 442–4). And long before July 1898 the *Idearium* had reached the hands of another young and fervent enquirer into Spanish destinies, Miguel de Unamuno, and was now resulting in the exchange of letters published in *El Defensor de Granada* under the title *El porvenir de España* (June–September 1898). In October Unamuno reviewed Ganivet's total production to date—five books—with warm appreciation (in *La Epoca*, 23 October 1898),[1] on 10 November Constantino Román Salamero informed Ganivet from Paris of progress with a French translation of the *Idearium* (AGM, p. 169), and a few days later *Cartas finlandesas* was the subject of an encouraging 'Palique' by Clarín (in *Madrid Cómico*, 19 November 1898).[2] Finally, at the time of Ganivet's death, two enthusiastic articles on him were in preparation: one by Rodrigo Soriano ('El misterioso granadino', published as part of *El Imparcial*'s obituary appreciation, 5 December 1898) and one by a French Hispanist, Léo Rouanet, for inclusion in *Revue Hispanique* (V, 1898, 483–95).

Despite a slight initial tardiness in recognition, then, literary and intellectual circles outside Granada were rather more prompt in proclaiming Ganivet's merits than has generally been suggested. At the time of his death, little more than two years after the publication of his first book, *Granada la bella*, little more than a year after the publication of *Idearium español*, Ganivet was clearly being accepted

[1] Also in Unamuno, *OC* V (Madrid 1952), 183–6.
[2] I assume this to be the 'Palique' that Saldaña and several later critics ascribe to an August number of *Los Lunes de El Imparcial* (QS, p. 95), for I have found no trace of Monday literary supplements in any of the three sets of *El Imparcial* that I have consulted for August 1898 (British Museum, Madrid Hemeroteca Municipal, Madrid Ateneo.) There are further Madrid notices/reviews of *Cartas finlandesas* in *Vida Nueva* (16 and 23 October 1898) and *Madrid Cómico* (12 November 1898).

as one of the most notable writers of the younger generation.

The acclaim of posterity

In the Epilogue to the *Libro de Granada* (1899) Nicolás María López noted that Ganivet's merits had been unanimously recognized after his death, and found satisfaction and pride in the knowledge that, by 'públicos y repetidos homenajes de admiración' Granada had recognized Ganivet's worth when he was almost unknown elsewhere. He continued:

> El fin inesperado y dolorosísimo de nuestro entrañable amigo, y la autoridad de un notable escritor madrileño, que lo quería como a un hermano, han fijado en él la distraída mirada del público, que ha tributado a su nombre los legítimos pero tristes resplandores de una gloria póstuma, que nosotros no pudimos darle, con nuestro humilde aplauso.[1]

The 'notable escritor madrileño' was Francisco Navarro Ledesma, Ganivet's most intimate friend in the Spanish capital, the author of several of the reviews already mentioned, and the most fervent champion of Ganivet in the weeks immediately following the latter's death: in *El Globo* (5 December 1898), in *La Revista Moderna* (10 December 1898),[2] and in *Los Lunes de El Imparcial* (13 February 1899). 'Desde que Navarro Ledesma publicó, en

---

[1] The Epilogue was not signed. Nicolás María López later declared his authorship in NML, p. 21.

[2] A large photo of Ganivet with a brief appreciation signed L. R. M. Since Francisco Navarro Ledesma was in charge of *La Revista Moderna*, it seems probable that Navarro himself wrote the appreciation and that L. R. M. stands simply for the title of the periodical. The style of the appreciation, too, suggests Navarro Ledesma: 'Angel Ganivet era el más genial y atrevido, el más sabio y fecundo, el más nuevo y sorprendente de cuantos ingenios jóvenes manejan la pluma en España.'

El Imparcial, su artículo "Fama póstuma",' wrote Nicolás María López in 1936, 'surgió una pléyade de admiradores entusiastas de Ganivet, que han sentido el ansia de interpretarlo y definirlo' (NML, p. 25).

But the 'pérdida irreparable' of Ganivet's death had been emphasized in lengthy articles several days before Navarro Ledesma made his own first obituary contribution: notably in *El Globo* on 1 December (in a 42-line front-page article) and in *El Imparcial* on 2 December (in a 73-line front-page article).[1] Consequently, one can perhaps best see Navarro Ledesma's contribution—and Rodrigo Soriano's (in *El Imparcial*, 5 December) and Nicolás María López's (in *Madrid Cómico*, 10 December)—as satisfying the press's need for immediate, first-hand knowledge of a writer whose greatness was sensed but whose work was still not widely known.

However, if the contributions of friends and admirers satisfied a need, they served also to exacerbate the public

[1] On the following Monday (5 December) *El Globo* devoted the whole of its *Plana del Lunes* to Ganivet, with the first of Navarro Ledesma's obituary appreciations and with extensive extracts from Ganivet's writings, and *El Imparcial* devoted two columns of its own literary supplement to him, with an article by Rodrigo Soriano and more extracts from Ganivet's writings. Other daily newspapers were rather less enterprising and the similarity of their reports with the recurrence of the words 'Cuantos han leído su *Idearium*, su *Pío Cid* y recientemente *Las cartas finlandesas*, han elogiado el talento original, el espíritu de observación y la vasta cultura del escritor' (in *El Liberal*, *El Nuevo País*, *El Correo*, *La Epoca*, *La Correspondencia de España*), suggests a scarcity of critics with ready knowledge of Ganivet's work. Nevertheless, considering Ganivet's recent incursion into Spanish letters, it is somewhat difficult to agree with Modesto Pérez that Ganivet, immediately after his death, received poor notices in the Spanish press (MP, 1920, p. xlii). 'Todos los periódicos lamentan su muerte y le rinden un tributo de admiración,' wrote Nicolás María López (in *Madrid Cómico*, 10 December 1898), and, with some exaggeration, 'todos los periódicos de la Corte, con unanimidad casi nunca vista, ni aun en la muerte de los hombres más ilustres, le dedican sentidos artículos necrológicos, reconociendo sus extraordinarias dotes intelectuales' (in *La Alhambra*, dated 30 November 1898, but the number appeared late because of the illness of the chief editor).

sense of loss and to draw attention to Ganivet's writings among a far wider public than they had hitherto enjoyed. Acclaim, it appears, followed immediately, and on 3 March 1899, only three months after Ganivet's death, we find Rubén Darío, then in Spain, referring to him as 'quizás la más adamantina concreción' of the new thought of the country, and observing:

> Ganivet no tenía enemigos, y por lo general, si conversáis con cualquiera de los intelectuales españoles, os dirá: 'Era el más brillante y el más sólido de todos los de su generación' (*España contemporánea*, Paris 1901, p. 84).

This fame, Rubén Darío felt, would inevitably grow as Ganivet's work became better understood, and in the same year, as though to confirm this prediction, a French scholar, Ephrem Vincent, published appreciative reviews of *Los trabajos* and of *Cartas finlandesas*,[1] and a German scholar, Hans Parlow, singled out Ganivet as the one great promise amidst the general barrenness and stagnation of contemporary Spanish literature.[2]

The seal of early recognition was fixed by the Ateneo of Madrid with an act of homage to Ganivet on the fifth anniversary of his death. Again the driving force behind the occasion was Francisco Navarro Ledesma, fulfilling an ambition that he had outlined almost five years before in a letter to Nicolás María López: to honour the anniversary of his friend's death with a collective tribute, 'como el compendio o muestra de lo que siente y piensa la juventud española'.[3] The occasion was widely and abundantly re-

[1] In *Mercure de France* XXIX (1899), 271–2, 834–5.
[2] 'Estado de la literatura española', in *Revista Nueva* II (August–December 1899), 145–58.
[3] Letter of 23 January 1899 (in NML, pp. 118–20). The aim, said Navarro, would be to publish a book on Ganivet by different young writers. Of the possible contributors mentioned in his letter, he, Una-

ported in the Spanish press. *El Imparcial* emphasized
Ganivet's profound influence on the new generations of
scholars (30 November 1903); *Alma Española* acclaimed
him as 'uno de los más hondos y originales espíritus de la
España contemporánea' (6 December 1903), and *Blanco y
Negro* as 'el pensador más profundo y el escritor más
original que produjo la tierra española en el siglo XIX'
(5 December 1903). Nor has posterity been less generous
in its praise, and scholars and critics of diverse political
and religious views have, decade after decade, contributed
their own variations on Navarro Ledesma's view of Ganivet as 'un hombre único y señero', 'precursor de razas
futuras',[1] and 'el más grande pensador moderno'.[2] Thus,
for Modesto Pérez, Ganivet was 'uno de nuestros más
grandes pensadores y literatos';[3] for Gómez de Baquero,
an 'hombre escogido' who joins with Unamuno and Costa
to form 'una trinidad de hombres geniales';[4] for Quintiliano Saldaña, 'una piedra miliaria que, en España, divide
los tiempos—como Cristo en el mundo';[5] 'el pensador

---

muno and Martínez Ruiz did eventually take part in the Ateneo *velada*,
together with Maeztu, who talked on 'Ganivet como político', and the
twenty-year-old Ortega y Gasset, who read Unamuno's study, 'Ganivet
filósofo', and a chapter from *Granada la bella* ('Nuestro carácter'). Later,
the contributions of Navarro, Unamuno and Martínez Ruiz (but not that
of Maeztu) were collected in book form (*Angel Ganivet*, Valencia 1905),
with the addition of a study by Constantino Román Salamero that had
first appeared, together with a report on the Ateneo *velada*, in the Madrid
daily *El País* (30 November 1903; with a different order of paragraphs).
Navarro Ledesma's enthusiastic panegyric was also published in
Helios (III, 1904, 45–57) and as the prologue to Ganivet's *Epistolario*
(Madrid 1904). Unamuno's study can now be most readily consulted in
his *Obras completas* (V, Madrid 1952, 210–14) and Martínez Ruiz's in
Azorín, *Obras completas* (VII, Madrid, 2nd ed., 1962, 206–11).

[1] *Angel Ganivet*, Valencia 1905, p. 12.
[2] *viva voce* to José Francés; cit. in *La Lectura* IV (1904), III, 449.
[3] MP, 1920, p. lxiii.
[4] *De Gallardo a Unamuno*, Madrid 1926, pp. 113, 110.
[5] QS, 1930, p. 190.

más actual y más español de los últimos tiempos,' affirmed
Juan del Rosal;[1] 'indudablemente,' Luis Rosales has
claimed, 'la primera figura de nuestro pensamiento desde
el siglo XVII a nuestros días'.[2] 'El interés por la persona y
la obra de Angel Ganivet no disminuye con el transcurso
del tiempo,' wrote Ricardo Gullón in 1953;[3] 'a cien años
de su nacimiento,' Antonio Gallego Morell has affirmed,
'Ganivet está más vigente que nunca'.[4]

And on what has this fame rested? Principally on *Idearium español*, the work which, according to Nicolás María
López, Ganivet himself doubtless held in highest esteem.[5]
'El *Idearium español*,' declared Román Salamero in the
homage of 1903, 'es un libro que sería constantemente
enaltecido si en otro país, que no fuera el nuestro, hubiera
aparecido'.[6] In fact, by 1903 the book was already receiv-
ing enthusiastic praise from many quarters and, in the
Ateneo *velada* itself, Ramiro de Maeztu singled it out
as Ganivet's best work and recommended its use as 'el
breviario de los parlamentarios españoles'.[7] Again posterity has echoed the praise of Ganivet's contemporaries. 'Es
una pura obra maestra,' wrote Maurice Legendre in 1909;[8]
'el más bello tratado de ciencia política de los tiempos
modernos,' added Angel del Arco in 1917;[9] '¡Qué magní-
fica síntesis de nuestra estructura nacional en sus varios
aspectos!' exclaimed Modesto Pérez in 1920; '¡qué honda
y bella condensación de los sucesos más notables de nuestro
país y de sus causas!'[10] For Gómez de Baquero it was 'el

---

[1] *Del pensar y vivir*, Madrid 1943, p. 23.
[2] Prologue to Angel Ganivet, *Antología*, Madrid 1943, p. xvi.
[3] In *Insula* 86 (February 1953).   [4] AGM, p. 187.
[5] In MP, 1920, p. 168, and NML, p. 126.
[6] In *El País*, 30 November 1903, and in *Angel Ganivet*, Valencia 1905,
p. 66.   [7] See the report in *El País*, 30 November 1903.
[8] In *La España Moderna*, May 1909, p. 133.
[9] In *La Alhambra* XX (1917), 302.   [10] MP, 1920, p. xvii.

más completo ensayo de la psicología del pueblo español de
su época';[1] for Rafael García y García de Castro, 'indudablemente el mejor libro de Ganivet y el que con
pleno derecho le ha colocado entre los pensadores
modernos más originales de nuestra patria';[2] for Antonio
Espina, 'sin comparacíon posible, el libro cumbre del
autor' and 'a no dudarlo [. . .], la obra central de todo el
sistema ganivetiano'.[3] 'No other book,' wrote Rafael
Martínez Nadal in 1946, 'has had so much influence—
whether by acceptance or rejection—on contemporary
Spanish thought and on foreign students of Spain.'[4]
Finally, in the centenary year, Melchor Fernández Almagro declared the *Idearium* to be 'un obligado punto de
referencia para cuantos pretendan adentrarse en la mis-
teriosa y concluyente España',[5] and Demetrio Castro
Villacañas, in a long and substantial series of articles,
emphasized the special relevance of the work to problems
of contemporary Spain.[6]

But what have critics and scholars found in Ganivet's
writings—and especially in his *Idearium*—that has filled
them with so much enthusiasm? The question is more
difficult to answer than it might at first appear, for despite
the chorus of praise indicated above, there have been
notable disagreements in the interpretation of Ganivet's
ideas and no Spanish writer has been proclaimed more
fervently during the last seventy years as a rallying-point
of such vastly different views. This has been especially

[1] In *El Sol*, 29 March 1925.
[2] *Los 'intelectuales' y la Iglesia*, Madrid 1934, p. 197.
[3] *Ganivet, el hombre y la obra* [1st ed., 1942], 3rd ed., Buenos Aires 1954,
pp. 33, 122.
[4] Introduction to Angel Ganivet, *Spain: An Interpretation*, London
1946, p. 9.   [5] In *El Libro Español* VIII (1965), 129.
[6] In sixteen articles published in *Los Domingos de Arriba*, 14 February
to 13 June 1965.

true in the field of politics, and because of its subsequent importance for my own study I devote the next section principally to this aspect of critical disagreement.

Ganivet in the Spanish political arena

We can pass quickly over the early years of critical disagreement—on the one hand, Ganivet the Europeanizer, unable to live in the 'caduca España del contenido medieval';[1] on the other, Ganivet the traditionalist, 'inspirado en lo más castizo y puro que encierra el alma española'[2]—and come immediately to March 1925 when the struggle between Right and Left for the possession of Angel Ganivet and the prestige of his name reached its climax, amidst the fervour of homage occasioned by the transfer of his mortal remains from Riga to Madrid and thence to his native Granada.

From the pages of the Catholic daily, *El Debate*, Nicolás González Ruiz decried the Leftish attempt to present Ganivet as though he had been a contributor to *El Liberal* or *La Voz*, and retorted with 'una breve antología de párrafos de Ganivet que podrían publicarse sin firma en *El Debate*' (25 March). On the following day an unnamed fellow collaborator to *El Debate* pressed the same point with greater vigour:

> Conviene en este caso opinar con claridad y con firmeza e ir contra la maquinación inadmisible que se está llevando a cabo. Se pretende que los restos de Angel Ganivet sirvan de bandera para una algarada izquierdista (26 March).

Not that the Right was slow to put forward its own misrepresentations—according to reports in the Socialist and

[1] From a poem by Luis Fernández Ardavín, read in the Madrid Ateneo on 21 January 1921 and reproduced in *El Sol* on the following day.

[2] NML, in MP, 1920, pp. 171-2. On this conflict see also Luis López Ballesteros, in *ABC* 10, 11, 16, 24, 25 October 1917.

Liberal press. Here, for example, is the review of a lecture
on Ganivet given by Professor Eduardo Ibarra in the
Catholic Student Residence in Madrid:

> Citó los párrafos de Ganivet en que aborda el problema
> de Marruecos, y tergiversándolos para adaptarlos a su con-
> veniencia, sostuvo que Ganivet dijo que España debe ir a
> Africa, no en son militar, sino en el de misioneros y pro-
> pagadores de la religión, primero, para que después la
> semilla cultural dé sus frutos.
> Claro es que Ganivet no dijo eso jamás en ninguna parte
> de su obra, y el discurso del Sr. Ibarra no es más que una
> breve muestra de cómo los elementos neos aprovechan
> cualquier coyuntura para defender sus doctrinas, aunque sea
> a costa de la verdad (*La Libertad*, 27 March).

And here is a brief extract from the same paper's report
of the act of homage in the University itself:

> No importa que los fariseos se apoderen por unas horas de
> una figura que nos pertenece y la esgriman hipócritamente
> para sus fines interesados. De rechazo, la algarabía nos bene-
> ficiará. Pasará el clamor ficticio, y Ganivet volverá a ser
> nuestro, únicamente nuestro; quedará totalmente restituido
> a nuestro culto (29 March).

A few voices of moderation were raised to emphasize
Ganivet's 'patriotismo inteligente', neither Right nor
Left, but they were drowned amidst the clamour of Right-
ish accusations of 'algarada izquierdista', Leftish accusations of 'torpeza derechista', and mutual accusations that
the other side had clearly never read Ganivet's writings. Conservatives found in the homage 'una prueba de
lo muy necesitada que se halla España de Gobiernos
fuertes', and Radicals took advantage of the occasion to
fling in the face of Primo de Rivera's Dictatorship their

declarations of faith in liberty and democracy. Eugenio
d'Ors, who had cast cold water on the basically radical act
of homage in the University by affirming in his address
the absurdity of presenting Ganivet as a representative
figure of the gathering's own feelings and desires,[1] subsequently reviewed the occasion in an article entitled,
appropriately, 'El arte de no aderezar los restos'. Classes,
he said, were suspended for the day but there was no need
for *enseñanzas* to be suspended as well. Ganivet was neither
progressive nor democratic nor liberal:

> ¿Por qué, pues, íbamos a empeñarnos, con escandaloso
> olvido de la moralidad científica impuesta por el carácter
> de la tribuna donde se hablaba, en *fabricar* un Ganivet a
> nuestro gusto, un Ganivet de convención pragmática y de
> mentira? ¿Por qué convocar su sombra para adular a la
> sombra del Parlamento—de lo que hizo aquí las veces de
> Parlamento—, y utilizar la presencia de unos puros despojos
> para mezclarlos con los mancillados despojos de la Consti-
> tución?
>
> ¡Cultive, en buena hora, la cocina burguesa el arte de
> aderezar los restos . . .! A mi entender, lo que la milicia in-
> telectual debe aprender en primer término—y practicar con
> valor de norma ante el ávido mirar de las juventudes—*es*,
> precisamente, *el arte de no aderezarlos* (*ABC*, 1 April).

But despite Eugenio d'Ors' objections and despite the
claims of the Right and the protests of more moderate
opinion, the repatriation of Ganivet's remains stands out
clearly as a triumph for the Left. It is the high-water mark

[1] See reports of the homage in the Spanish press (29 March), notably
in the Monarchist daily, *ABC*, which in general eschewed the extremist
clamours of Right and Left, and emphasized more conciliatory views
of Ganivet: 'el profundo error de quienes tratan de considerarle un
apasionado por tendencias de la derecha o de la izquierda' (27 March);
'no lo pueden levantar como pendón ni los radicales ni los reaccionarios'
(29 March).

of Ganivet's fame as a liberal and a democrat. Thereafter, the tide turns, and Eugenio d'Ors' article can be seen as a pointer. But an extremely critical study of the *Idearium* by Manuel Azaña, in turn premier and president of the Second Republic, doubtless exerted a greater influence.[1] At all events, during the 1930's Ganivet was gradually abandoned by the Left and held up increasingly as a champion of authoritarianism. As examples I take two studies published in Germany in 1940: the first by Francisco Elías de Tejada, who purports to find in Ganivet an unwitting Carlist, and the second by Pedro Laín Entralgo, who seeks to demonstrate Ganivet's relevance to National Syndicalism.

The approach to Ganivet, says Elías de Tejada, 'no es un problema de discurso, sino una cuestión de sentimiento' (p. 175).[2] He himself did not understand Ganivet properly, he confesses, until 'los días ardientes y místicos de aquel verano guerrero de 1936', when he found a half-burnt copy of the *Idearium* in Torrijos and came to realize that Ganivet, too, like himself, would have been a soldier of the Caudillo, as he was also 'un mártir de la barbarie roja' (pp. 175–6).[3] The author then reviews briefly the various conflicting views of Ganivet and gives his support to those writers who have found in him an upholder of

[1] *Plumas y palabras*, Madrid 1930, pp. 9–115 ('El *Idearium* de Ganivet'). Azaña had published the first part of his study in 1921, under the pen-name Cardenio ('En torno a Ganivet', in *La Pluma*, February 1921, pp. 87–96), but at that time he was known only as a writer and an intellectual, and his article apparently did nothing to lessen anyone's enthusiasm for Ganivet. Perhaps the pen becomes mightier when one holds a sword as well.
[2] Francisco Elías de Tejada y Spínola, 'Para interpretar a Angel Ganivet', in *Ensayos y Estudios* (Instituto Ibero-Americano de Berlín) II (1940), 175–89. The article is a summary of the author's findings in his book of the previous year, *Ideas políticas de Angel Ganivet*, Madrid 1939.
[3] A reference to the alleged order by the 'Gobierno Rojo' in Valencia that the *Idearium* be withdrawn from its libraries.

Spanish tradition, for it is these, he declares, who have
studied Ganivet most deeply (pp. 176–8). Thereupon,
after affirming as a necessary preliminary to his arguments
'el valor del ideario carlista', he sets out to show that
Ganivet's 'ideario coincide con el del Carlismo' (p. 179):

> el alma española que en él [Ganivet] late le lleva de un modo
> fatal e irremediable a propugnar los ideales de España, esto
> es, a los de aquel grupo que representaba la esencia de lo
> español en el siglo XIX: el Carlismo guerrero y militante (pp.
> 179–80).

The author considers in turn Ganivet's attitude to 'el
aspecto religioso' ('su postura última es la misma que la de
los hombres de la boina roja', p. 182), to 'la cuestión
política' (here also Angel Ganivet, he finds, 'está bajo las
banderas de la Tradición de las Españas', p. 185) and to
'la forma del gobierno' ('Ganivet intuía, al menos, y
llevaba en el corazón, el tercero de los postulados del
Carlismo', p. 187). Only the prejudices of Ganivet's education and environment and his early departure from
Spain before he had attained full intellectual maturity pre-
vented his professing openly the truths that he arrived at
through intuition:

> El alma de Ganivet no está en unas frases hueras sin
> sentido, sino en el estudio de su obra y en el palpitar al
> unísono con las ambiciones de su corazón, creyendo que lo
> español es cosa aparte y superior a las demás del mundo.
> Así, y sólo así, se explica su adscripción intuitiva a la
> gloriosa Tradición española. Por eso, sin ser católico, es
> intransigente fanático; sin ser fuerista, pide un regionalismo
> a la usanza tradicional; y sin ser carlista militante, postula la
> monarquía federativa como el único ideal posible (pp. 188–
> 189).

The author concludes his article—and sums up his view—with a quotation from his book, *Ideas políticas de Angel Ganivet*:

> Carlista sin saberlo, quizás porque no supo a ciencia cierta lo que el Carlismo era, [Ganivet] marcó todos sus actos con el sello santo de la Hispanidad auténtica, y supo legarnos un camino y una guía, que son, para gloria imperecedora de su nombre y de su genio, el camino de la Tradición española y la guía luminosa de la raíz íntima de España (p. 189).

Laín Entralgo, in a rather more searching article, considers the relevance of Ganivet's thought to the National-Syndicalist ideals of his own day.[1]

In the first section of his study, 'Actualidad de Ganivet' (pp. 67-73), he claims that Ganivet, with his typically Spanish insistence on 'la exaltación senequista de la humana dignidad' (p. 71), offers a solution to the danger of modern man's enslavement to technology. But National-Syndicalist youth, he affirms, must not scorn technology as Ganivet does. 'La fe, católica y patria, exige la técnica y su misionera difusión: propaganda. . .' (p. 73). Ganivet, in common with others of his generation, is content merely to observe; 'en todos faltó el genio fundacional y apostólico que transfigurase la psicología en destino, la costumbre en impetuosa historia' (p. 72).[2]

---

[1] P. Laín Entralgo, 'Visión y revisión del *Idearium español* de Angel Ganivet', in *Ensayos y Estudios* (Instituto Ibero-Americano de Berlín) II (1940), 67-93. This article was subsequently republished, under the title 'Tres notas y un pico sobre el *Idearium español*', as the prologue to Laín's edition of the *Idearium* (Ediciones 'Fe', Madrid 1942).

[2] Nevertheless, Laín Entralgo's apparent desire to enlist Ganivet in his crusade does cause him at moments to misinterpret what Ganivet says, as for example when he claims that Ganivet really desired 'la técnica' and lamented the lack of technical reflexion in Spanish painters (p. 70). Apart from some confusion on Laín's part between 'técnica' in the sense

c

In the next section, 'Senequismo, hispanismo y cristianismo' (pp. 74–84), Laín Entralgo distinguishes between
'senequismo como invariante histórica española' (in which
he believes Ganivet to be mistaken) and 'senequismo como
ingrediente de costumbre' (in which he believes him to
be right) (p. 78). He believes, then, that the important
senequismo for Spain is not the total, integrated, individual
system of Seneca himself, but that which reveals itself as
a recurrent attitude to problems characterizing 'el tipo
español' across the centuries (for example, in the form
taken by Christianity in Spain). Now if I understand Laín
Entralgo's thought correctly, he is here seeking to relax
the imperious determinism of Ganivet's *senequismo*, and to
transform it into a mere characteristic attitude ('costumbre') that is then capable of further transformation
into 'impetuosa historia' (cf. the last quotation in my preceding paragraph). Similarly, later in the section he praises
Ganivet for demanding a passion of unity, but laments
his 'nacionalismo casticista' according to which Spain
should continue in her humility instead of universalizing
her ideas by projection beyond merely national frontiers.
'*Sólo* hubo místicos españoles,' Laín Entralgo reminds us,
'cuando España hablaba al mundo su universal lenguaje
de hierro y teologías' (p. 81).

In the third and final section of his study, 'Alma e
historia de España' (pp. 84–93), the author aims to 'en-
frentar los postulados ganivetianos en orden al ser y al
destino de España con el sentido nacionalsindicalista de

---

of *technology* and 'técnica' in the sense of *technique*, it seems that here also
Ganivet simply stated and accepted rather than 'lamented':
  Lo más interesante en estas anomalías que de nuestro carácter provie-
  nen, es que no hay medio de evitarlas, imitando los buenos modelos
  y formando escuelas artísticas; nosotros no queremos imitar; pero,
  aunque quisiéramos, no podríamos hacerlo con fruto (217).

ese ser y de ese destino' (p. 84). His basic criticism is the
same as in his previous sections: Ganivet tells us only
what Spain *is* ('sujeta al *pedigree* de los españoles', p. 89)
and not what Spain *can be*. Nevertheless, Ganivet, he finds,
had a remarkable insight into Spanish psychology and in
many cases his words call to mind others spoken by José
Antonio and the Caudillo. But Spanish character, as he
reveals it, must not be abandoned to mere 'proceso natural
[. . .] como parecía querer Ganivet'; it must become the
basis of historical action (p. 92); historicism must yield to
an act of faith (p. 93).[1]

The present study

Ganivet the champion of *europeísmo*, or Ganivet the
staunch traditionalist? Ganivet the upholder of Spain's
mission in Africa, or Ganivet the advocate of Spain's
withdrawal from such involvements? Ganivet the Democrat, or Ganivet the Falangist? Ganivet the Socialist, or
Ganivet the Carlist? And to venture for a moment outside
the field of politics: Ganivet the 'católico de pura cepa',[2]
or Ganivet the non-catholic, 'digan ahora lo que quieran
quienes no lo han leído'?[3] Ganivet of whom it was said
that 'ni su personalidad literaria ni sus ideas están forma-
das',[4] or Ganivet the mature writer, 'totalmente hecho y
[que] ofrece en su pensamiento y en su literatura una
sorprendente madurez'?[5] Ganivet whose *Idearium* and

---

[1] The relevance of Ganivet's *Idearium* to the aims and ideals of the
Falange has since been urged on several occasions, notably by Luis
Furones Ferrero (in *Seminarios* 5, March–April 1961, 145–50; 6, May–
June 1961, 83–93) and by Demetrio Castro Villacañas (in *Los Domingos
de Arriba*, sixteen articles, 14 February to 13 June 1965).

[2] MP, 1918, p. 200.

[3] Américo Castro, in *El Sol*, 29 March 1925.

[4] NML, Prologue to *Cartas finlandesas*, Granada 1898, pp. li-lii.

[5] AGM, p. 14.

Porvenir de España 'anticiparon, con calor y luz de pro-
fecía, nuestros años presentes',[1] or Ganivet who 'fracasó
en casi todos sus pronósticos'?[2] Ganivet whose originality
astounds one,[3] or Ganivet whose lack of originality reduces the importance of the *Idearium*?[4] The extent of
critical disagreement is truly alarming. So is the blatant
anthologizing of Ganivet's writings to adapt them to
party passions and prejudices, and the arrogant disregard
or over-facile rejection of points that cannot be adapted,
and—amidst so much critical disagreement—the eager
advocacy of the *Idearium* (that is, of one's own interpretation of the *Idearium*) as a true guide to national action. In
certain quarters, it appears, Eugenio d'Ors' admonition is
still depressingly relevant: '¿Por qué [vamos] a empeñar-
nos, con escandaloso olvido de la moralidad científica
[. . .], en *fabricar* un Ganivet a nuestro gusto?'

The questions raised by so much disagreement are
numerous. For example, what have writers of such different political views found in the *Idearium* that has made
them so eager to enlist its author in their various bands?
And to what extent is Ganivet himself responsible for so
much conflict of opinion? Is it perhaps the result of his
much emphasized 'espíritu genuinamente asistemático'?[5]
'No tenía pensamiento político claro,' says one critic;[6]
'Nada más claro [. . .] que su sistema político,' affirms
another.[7] And this last disagreement suggests yet another

[1] Antonio Gallego Burín, in *La Estafeta Literaria*, 10 August 1944.
[2] Antonio Espina, in *La Estafeta Literaria*, 10 August 1944.
[3] Luis Rosales, Prologue to Ángel Ganivet, *Antología*, [Madrid] 1943,
p. xvi.
[4] Pedro Rocamora, 'Ganivet y su *Idearium* desde otro siglo', in *Arbor*
Nos. 237-8 (September–October 1965), p. 11.
[5] MFA, 'Ángel Ganivet (1865–1898),' in *El Libro Español* VIII (1965),
129.   [6] E. Gómez de Baquero, in *El Sol*, 7 April 1925.
[7] Luis Rosales, Prologue to Angel Ganivet, *Antología*, [Madrid] 1943,
p. x.

question: Is it a merit or a demerit that the *Idearium* should allow so many differences of interpretation? 'The very fact that now and then Ganivet has been quoted by all parties, from the traditionalists to the typically Spanish anarchists,' says R. M. Nadal, 'is a clear proof of his freedom from party dogmatism, and of his tacit acceptance of the good that is in each one of them.'[1] Diversity of critical interpretation has been invoked frequently as evidence of the greatness of a work of literature. But can this apply in the present case? And to extend the question of merit and demerit still further, what is the *Idearium* really worth as a probing of the problem of Spain? Is it the masterpiece that most critics have suggested, or were Ortega y Gasset, Manuel Azaña, Ramón Gómez de la Serna and, recently, Pedro Rocamora nearer the truth in their own less favourable views?[2]

Before we can consider these questions we must look more closely at the work itself. 'Angel Ganivet,' wrote Melchor Fernández Almagro in the introduction to his celebrated study of 1925, 'es más admirado que conocido.' There has been no lack of enthusiastic praise, he continued; what is lacking is 'estudio objetivo y sereno'.[3] Similar points have been made repeatedly during the forty-odd years since Fernández Almagro's book first appeared. 'Muy a pesar de sus [Ganivet's] brillantes éxitos, no ha sido aún comprendida la importancia de su labor'

---

[1] Introduction to Angel Ganivet, *Spain: An Interpretation*, London 1946, p. 23.

[2] José Ortega y Gasset, in *Faro* (Madrid), 9 August 1908 ('tengo [de Ganivet] una opinión muy distinta de la común entre los jóvenes, pero que me callo por no desentonar inútilmente'); Manuel Azaña, see above, p. 25, n. 1; Ramón Gómez de la Serna, in *La Tribuna*, 31 January and 2 February 1921 (reproduced in his book *Azorín* [1st ed. 1930], Buenos Aires 1942, pp. 115–22); Pedro Rocamora, in *Arbor* Nos. 237–8 (September-October 1965), pp. 5–17.

[3] MFA, *Vida y obra de Angel Ganivet*, Valencia [1925], pp. 8–9.

(1943);[1] 'siendo uno de los pensadores españoles modernos más citados, sigue siendo una figura sin estudiar' (1952);[2] Ganivet gives to his generation 'soluciones aún no estudiadas con la atención y claridad debidas' (1957);[3] 'Ganivet [. . .] no ha sido comprendido en lo que de más profundo encerró su obra' (1965).[4] Despite the appearance, over the years, of a number of valuable and searching studies on Ganivet and his writings, there is some justification for making the point yet again at the beginning of yet another study. But my own aim is more limited than that of most of my predecessors who have written at length on Ganivet, and my approach rather different, for I do not seek in this study to embrace the author's whole production. Instead, I shall concentrate on a single work, the *Idearium*, and refer to his other writings only when I find them especially relevant to the *Idearium*. It is my hope that by the close study of this one work I shall come near to a proper understanding of Ganivet as a man and a writer. But this is not my main concern. My chief aim is simply to study and evaluate *Idearium español*.

[1] Luis Rosales, Prologue to Angel Ganivet, *Antología*, [Madrid] 1943, p. vii.

[2] Constantino Láscaris Comneno, in *Revista de la Universidad de Buenos Aires* XX (1952), 453.

[3] Joaquín de Entrambasaguas, in *Las mejores novelas contemporáneas*, I, Barcelona 1957, 1127.

[4] Luis Aguirre Prado, *Ganivet*, Madrid 1965, p. 28.

II

IDEARIUM ESPAÑOL: EXPOSITION

My aim in this chapter is one of simple exposition: to indicate as briefly and as clearly as possible the essential lines of Ganivet's thought as it reveals itself in *Idearium español*. It is an elementary task, but in view of the elementary misinterpretations to which Ganivet's work has been subjected, it is perhaps not a completely superfluous one. Many of the disagreements indicated in my previous chapter have arisen, I believe, from careless reading of the *Idearium* and from the failure to grasp Ganivet's thought as an integrated whole. His words have too often been torn from their context and flourished as banners of party passions. My emphasis in the following pages, then, is on Ganivet's thought as a system. I shall start with a mere summary of his book and thereafter emphasize what I find to be its basic ideas.

OUTLINE OF THE WORK[1]

A. [*'fuerzas constituyentes del alma de* [*España*]*'* (*209*)]

151: The fervour with which the dogma of the Immaculate Conception has been upheld in Spain must reflect something of the Spanish soul and of Spanish life: an ideal of virginity maintained amidst the imposed duty of motherhood.

---

[1] I emphasize with a footnote that my aim in this first section is one of simple, dispassionate summary. Except for the occasional [bracketed] comment, the ideas and illustrations—and even the terminology (for example, Charles I for Charles V)—are Ganivet's own.

151–73: The essential basis of the whole moral being of
Spain is to be found in a Senecan type of stoicism that
says, 'Remain true to your own inner, indestructible self
whatever the outside pressures on you.' This *senequismo*
has had an incalculable influence in many different spheres
of Spanish life. As a system of morality it proclaimed the
exhaustion of Graeco-Roman philosophy and, with its
'doctrinas nobles, justas y humanitarias' (155), prepared
the way for Christianity, which in turn developed its own
philosophy, with local variations. In Spain the Church
acquired its especially imperious power because of the
weakness of the Visigoths and it took over effective
control of the country in temporal as well as ecclesiastical
matters. This marks the birth of the Catholic State. But
despite its great social power, religion did not develop in
energy and depth of feeling, and Christian thought revealed itself only as a sort of embryonic Scholasticism
common to other Christian countries besides Spain. But
then came the Arabic invasions, which gave the Spanish
spirit its outlet in action and in popular poetry inspired by
that action. Moreover, from the long Arabic occupation,
with the resulting contacts and conflicts, were born the
most notable tendencies of the Spanish religious spirit:
mysticism and fanaticism, Santa Teresa and the *autos de fe*.
The effeminate logic-chopping of the Scholastics, aimed
at centralization and universalization, pales beside the
virile passions of Christianity in action. If it is to exert real
influence on people's lives, Christian philosophy must not
seek to be universal and absolute; it must be based on the
life of each individual people. Imposed unity can only
disguise diversity; it cannot prevent it. Hitherto there has
been too much insistence in Spain on unity by force and
not enough on intellectual debate. But debate would not

cause Spain to be diverted from her true course; it would serve only to prompt awareness of where that true course lies. In short, Spain needs a dissident minority in order to make the rest react with a new consciousness of their true tradition.

173–81: In a psychological study the difficulty is to bring together in a logical scheme both inner experience and external phenomena. Similarly, in studying the psychological structure of a country one must look for the essential nucleus to which all external phenomena are related. That nucleus is to be found in the 'espíritu territorial' (175), which is formed by the geological disposition of the country. As there are islands, continents and peninsulas, so also there is an island spirit, a continental spirit and a peninsular spirit, and each one allows variations according to more particular relationships. The general principle is the same in all cases, self-preservation, but this manifests itself differently in the different geological formations: by aggression in islands, by resistance in continents, and by independence in peninsulas. Thus, England is a typical island nation and its history has been one of constant aggression; France is an example of a continental nation and its wars have been merely frontier wars (except with Napoleon, who was a foreigner and an islander, and since Napoleon because of his influence); Spain is a peninsular nation and its history is an unending series of invasions and expulsions, 'una guerra permanente de independencia' (181).

181–7: But Spain has also been aggressive. Why? Ganivet attributes it to a transformation of the native spirit of independence brought about during the Reconquest. The Christian kingdoms of the north wished to expel the Arabs, but their spirit of independence made

them jealous of one another and when Castile, because of
its central position, eventually predominated, Portugal
and Aragon-Catalonia-Valencia were driven to affirming
their independence within the Peninsula by action without
(the former in maritime exploration, the latter in Mediterranean politics and diplomacy). Castile itself then became an aggressive power out of rivalry, and the forces
that should have gone against Africa were diverted to the
New World. Castile's economic revival was impossible
with the loss of so much labour. But aggression was
a deviation from the country's true being, a transformation of the territorial spirit. As such, it remains
superficial and destined to disappear with the policy that
bred it.

[Now we can understand the significance of Ganivet's
opening paragraph. He considers that the dogma he there
describes is fervently proclaimed in Spain because it is an
intimate reflection of Spain's own life: (1) Spain, too, has
within her an ideal of virginity (that is, her territorial spirit
of independence); (2) Spain, too, has had imposed upon
her the duty of motherhood (that is, the distraction into
imperial exploits); (3) Spain, too, has accepted that duty
but now must come to realize that 'su espíritu era ajeno a
su obra' (151) and rediscover her own true inner self (the
territorial spirit of independence again). In the remaining
pages of Section A Ganivet will consider three different
spheres of activity—military (187-99), legal (199-208) and
artistic (209-22)—, and try to show how the peculiarly
Spanish reaction to these things confirms his findings on
Spanish character and how these findings point to practical solutions.]

187-99: There is an important difference between
espíritu guerrero and *espíritu militar*: one is spontaneous and

the other reflective, one is in man and the other in society, one is a striving against organization and the other a striving for organization. Spain, because of her territorial spirit of independence, is essentially a warrior nation, not a military nation, and her history is one of unorganized fighting and small combat units (Viriato, the Cid, the Gran Capitán, the Conquistadores, Cervantes in Algiers, San Ignacio de Loyola; Ganivet here champions the hand-to-hand skirmisher against the mechanized, long-distance killer, and prefers the money-lender to the banker, the owner-occupier to the large property magnate, the cobbler to the shoe-manufacturer). When there is armed conflict in Spain, all the social classes rise up to take over the direction of the war. Individual action of this type should not be condemned but encouraged because it is in harmony with the Spanish territorial spirit. And the Spanish army should be composed of small combat units that can be joined together if necessary into a single force but which will operate principally in isolation.

199–208: Nowhere is there so great a contrast between the purity of an ideal and the crude impurity of reality as in the field of justice, and the legal spirit of a given country is discovered in the relationship that exists there between the ideal and the reality. On the one hand, then, there is the prosaic, practical system of written laws (which in Spain is a complex of elements brought from outside) and, on the other, there is the 'ley ideal superior' (200) in the light of which those written laws are interpreted—or misinterpreted. 'Un criterio jurídico práctico' follows out the laws impartially, however the notion of pure justice may suffer; 'un criterio jurídico idealista' makes written rules conform to a higher justice (201). Because of the combined influence of Christian feeling and

Senecan morality, Spain is characterized by an idealistic approach to legal matters, and the Spaniard's exalted notion of justice reveals itself both in the rigorous pursuit of immorality and in the lenience shown to offenders, both in the harshness of the country's legal code and in the frequent use of the pardon. Cervantes separated the two forms of justice—the ideal and the practical—in the figures of Don Quixote and Sancho, and in history it was the native Quixotic tendency to judge in the light of a higher justice that caused the Castilian people to choose Isabella (and union with Aragon) rather than Juana la Beltraneja (and union with Portugal). [Here Ganivet makes no practical recommendation, but his view appears to be that Spaniards must continue to act as in the past.]

209-22: Though Spain has inherited the same threefold tradition as other European nations—Christian religion, Greek art and Roman law—, the particular combination that Spain has made is different from that made by other countries because the climate and the race are different. Spain's spirit is primarily religious and artistic, and it is religion especially, in its supreme form, mysticism, that finds expression in Spanish art. But the manner of that expression, too, is important and again it is a reflection of fundamental Spanish character, namely, the territorial spirit of independence, which shows itself in the artist's lack of technical preoccupations and in his resolution to be guided only by the impulse of his own genius. Sometimes, when the artist is a Velázquez or a Goya, a Lope or a Cervantes, the result is an inimitable masterpiece; at other times, it is a mere bungling. We neither like imitation nor does the 'excesiva fuerza personal' (217) of our great works permit it, so that our art has to be renewed periodically from abroad. Writers should be encouraged to remain under the steadying influence of their own regional environments. Too much Spanish energy has been squandered in the quest for glory. But for wars and colonization, the Golden Age would have been far greater than it was.

B. [*Spain's external policy: history and proposal*]

223-33: Spain's foreign policy in modern times has operated in four directions: north, south, east and west. Castile's policy was southern and it was logical that after the fall of Granada our reply to Moslem aggression should be carried into Africa. Aragonese policy was eastern and, as Aragon helped Castile in its southern policy, so Castile joined with Aragon in its Italian enterprises. The discovery of America added western interests and the accession of Charles I brought involvement in northern, European affairs. Of these four directions of foreign policy, the first two, those towards Africa and Italy, were 'natural and justified' (225), the third had some justification in our character, our faith and in the workings of providence, but the last one, the continental policy, was an 'immeasurable political absurdity' (226) because it went against our natural, peninsular character. Charles I, a continental monarch, submitted Spain to his own personal policy and made it serve his ends, but with Philip II, a Spanish king, the consequences of a peninsular mentality applied to a continental situation were to be disastrous. Nor were the Bourbons any better than the Habsburgs in seeing where the real, permanent interests of the country lay.

234-77: These four directions of foreign policy still live on today. How should we see ourselves in relation to them?

Northern (*i.e. European*) *policy* (235–44). This fatal policy is completely 'exhausted, dead and buried' (235) and Spain must not allow herself to become involved again in a policy foreign to her territorial spirit. We must recognize the *status quo*, even over Gibraltar and over peninsular disunity (that is, the separate existence of Spain and Portugal).

Western (*i.e. Latin American*) *policy* (244–56). The nations of Latin America have inherited the Spanish spirit of independence. Consequently, they have rebelled against Spanish rule and insisted on starting again from the beginning. Unlike the United States, then, which imported European experience, Latin American countries are still in a state of excessive, ill-controlled, childhood vitality. Moreover, they regard with suspicion any intervention by Spain in the political and economic field. Spain must therefore avoid Ibero-American unions, and concentrate on re-establishing her intellectual prestige, even though this means accepting foreign influences. She must then strive to implant that prestige in Latin America, offering intellectual guidance freely and in a sense of real brotherhood.

Eastern (*i.e. Mediterranean*) *policy* (256–66). Spain is very much concerned with Mediterranean politics, especially with questions concerning the temporal power of the Papacy and the Turkish domination in Eastern Europe. Nevertheless, our situation and our history show us that in neither case would Spanish intervention be in the national interests. Moreover, our intervention would be a disservice to the very causes we should be striving to serve.

(266–73: An interlude in which Ganivet emphasizes Spain's need for internal recuperation, especially spiritual and intellectual recuperation, as a basis for the strengthening of Spanish prestige in Latin America. Foreign influences can be accepted, but they must be adapted to the fundamental, inevitable, traditional spirit of Spain.)

Southern (*i.e. African*) *policy* (273–7). At the end of the Reconquest it was natural and logical that Spain should carry the war into Africa, and an indestructible political power would have been established. But times have changed; now it is too late.

[In short, Spain is not summoned to foreign adventures in any direction, and her peninsular character makes such adventures inadvisable. Spain's material strength must not be squandered on the world; it must be aimed at internal recuperation. Still more important, Spain needs a great intellectual revival. Foreign influences will play their part but they must be integrated into Spain's own tradition, and any revival must be based on a proper understanding of this tradition and of Spain's place in the modern world. With her intellectual prestige re-established in this way, Spain must allow the countries of Latin America to draw freely on her intellectual store. She will thereby maintain and strengthen her spiritual leadership of the Hispanic peoples.]

C. [*Towards the spiritual regeneration of Spain*]

278–86: Spain, like Segismundo, was snatched from obscurity and plunged into a fantastic life of action. Now we have returned to our misery and our poverty. We must strengthen our organization and develop our intellectual resources; we must forge new spiritual ideals capable of bringing together and of guiding the Hispanic peoples. At present the frontiers of Spain are open to conflicting doctrines from abroad, and these doctrines continue to coexist in conflict in our Universities. We must rethink them seriously, independently, for ourselves, within the context of our own traditions. In this way, the destructive external action to which the whole nation now aspires will be transformed into creative internal action, and our institutions will be given their most appropriate form.

286–94: But at present Spain is suffering from *abulia*, which consists in a debilitation of the will when faced by new and conflicting ideas. Sometimes we seize on one idea; sometimes on another; often we live simply by recalling the past. We fail to synthesize; we fail to see ideas in their proper perspective; we lack the stimulus of healthy, productive ideas such as result from serious study and reflection. Our thought is ill-defined, our true interests unrecognized, our activity undirected and therefore inadequate. Hitherto, we have been too ready for action. One should think before acting. Let us think.

295–305: Spain needs, above all, to be spiritually restored. This calls for education, but not by the present system which is based on memory training. Individual, independent intellectual work must be encouraged; differing and conflicting ideas must be studied and discussed instead of being converted directly into action. The Arabic invasions gave Spain her most energetic individualism, and as this energetic individualism once sent us off on foreign adventures, so it is waiting now to be converted into inner creativeness and to send us off on our true course of intellectual greatness. Don Quixote is our guide, in his freedom from material preoccupations and in his endless, idealizing creativity. We must follow him and realize our great spiritual triumph, 'porque, al renacer, hallaremos una inmensidad de pueblos hermanos a quienes marcar con el sello de nuestro espíritu' (305).

THE APPROACH TO SPAIN

In *Idearium español* Ganivet is concerned with the problem of Spain: her greatness in the past, her apparent decadence in the present, and the means of her regeneration in the future. Before examining his findings, we must consider how he views civilization and thence how he approaches the problem of Spain. I find a key to his approach in the following passage:

> Para que la filosofía cristiana no sea una fórmula conven-cional, para que ejerza influencia real en la vida de los hombres, es preciso que arranque de esa misma vida, como las leyes, como el arte. Una legislación, un arte cosmopolita, son nubes de verano; y una filosofía universal, como pre-tendió serlo la escolástica, es contraproducente. Someter a la acción de una ideología invariable la vida de pueblos diversos, de diversos orígenes e historia, solo puede con-ducir a que esa ideología se transforme en una etiqueta, en un rótulo, que den una unidad aparente debajo de la cual se escondan las energías particulares de cada pueblo, dis-puestas siempre a estallar, y a estallar con tanta más violencia cuanto más largo haya sido el periodo de forzado silencio. La filosofía más importante, pues, de cada nación es la suya propia, aunque sea muy inferior a las imitaciones de ex-trañas filosofías: lo extraño está sujeto a alternativas, es asunto de moda, mientras que lo propio es permanente, es el cimiento sobre el que se debe construir, sobre el que hay que construir cuando lo artificial se viene abajo (166-7).

For Ganivet, philosophy, laws and art are not universal and absolute, equally valid for all peoples. In dealing

D

with a civilization one is not operating upon a blank sheet; there is no *tabula rasa*; each nation has its own individual life, its own character, its own history. For a philosophy to have real influence in a country, for legislation to prosper, for art to flourish, each must be firmly rooted in the particular, individual being of the people of that country. Systems imposed from outside neglect and suppress national energies; they are artificial; they cannot last. There is, says Ganivet,—and there must be—a close connection between the character of a nation and the character of its civilization. Since nations differ, so also civilizations differ. Yet we appear afraid of probing beneath external appearances of unity; 'estamos dominados por la manía de la unificación' (167). We forget that whatever outside appearances may suggest, inner diversity is inevitable: 'Las unidades aparentes y convencionales no pueden destruir la diversidad real de las cosas; no sirven más que para encubrirla' (168).

'Sería, pues, muy fecundo y en ninguna manera peligroso romper la unidad filosófica' (170). An individual nation should not accept any system of thought or belief in its absolutism and its totality; every system should be rethought on the basis of the nation's own particular character:

> Hay, pues, muchos modos de servir al ideal, y a cada hombre se le debe pedir solo que lo sirva según su natural comprensión, y a cada pueblo, que lo entienda según su propio genio (210).

So it was with Spain's inheritance from Antiquity:

> Nuestras ideas, si se atiende a su origen, son las mismas que las de los demás pueblos de Europa, los cuales, con mejor o peor derecho, han sido partícipes del caudal hereditario

legado por la antigüedad; pero la combinación que nosotros hemos hecho de esas ideas es nuestra, propia y exclu-
siva, y es diferente de la que han hecho los demás, por ser
diferentes nuestro clima y nuestra raza (211).

So it was with Christianity which took on different characteristics in different parts of the Roman Empire:

> Esa evolución [of Christianity], sin embargo, no fue igual ni
> pudo serlo en las diversas provincias del Imperio romano
> [. . .]; hubo divergencias nacidas de la variedad de tempera-
> mentos y acentuadas gradualmente conforme los cambios
> históricos iban dando vida a nuevos rasgos característicos y
> diferenciadores (157-8).

So it must be with the future restoration of Spain:

> En cuanto a la restauración ideal, nadie pondrá en duda que
> debe ser obra nuestra exclusiva; podremos recibir influen-
> cias extrañas, orientarnos estudiando lo que hacen y dicen
> otras naciones; pero mientras no españolicemos nuestra
> obra, mientras lo extraño no esté sometido a lo español y
> vivamos en la incertidumbre en que hoy vivimos, no levan-
> taremos cabeza (267).

Each nation has its own individual character and an
element of civilization common to several nations takes
on different forms according to the different character of
each one of them. Ganivet believes it proper that this
should be so. Similarly, an element of civilization taken
by one nation from another must be remoulded to the
character of the adopting nation. Attempts to suppress
national character by imposing ready-made solutions
from outside will simply deform and debilitate the
country, forcing it along paths for which it is unsuited.
Furthermore, forms and solutions imposed from outside
will inevitably come into conflict with those demanded by

the nation's own fundamental being and, in suppressing them, will prepare the way for violence, 'y [. . .] tanta más violencia cuanto más largo haya sido el periodo de forzado silencio' (167). 'Un poder que no brota espontáneo de la fuerza natural y efectiva de una nación', says Ganivet, 'es un palo en manos de un ciego' (257-8). If, on the other hand, a nation transforms what it receives from outside, adapting it to its own individual being, that nation will prosper and be strong and there will be no grounds for conflict. Thus, in the field of religion Spain has adapted Christianity so completely to herself, she is so 'fused with her religious ideal' (171), that there can be no fear from heretics. Spain has the form of religion most suited to her; heretics would even make a valuable contribution to the nation by stimulating awareness of this fact. In short: a country, like a person, has a particular psychological structure, a particular character; a country that struggles against or is forced to act against its own native character weakens itself; a country that lives at one with its character prospers.

So far I have been showing how, for Ganivet, a given element of civilization will—or at least should—take on different forms in different countries. And, of course, there is a corollary to this: just as a common element of civilization will take on different forms in different countries, so also different elements of civilization will—or at least should—tend towards common forms within the same country. For they are (or become) part of the same tradition; they are marked by the same national character; 'todo está fundido en la personalidad nacional' (225). The 'personalidad nacional', then, must be the basic concern of the student of civilization. And within that 'personalid nacional', he will seek especially the all-

pervading 'fuerza dominante y céntrica' (211), 'el núcleo
irreducible al que están adheridas todas las envueltas que
van transformando en el tiempo la fisonomía de ese país'
(175). Once one has established this 'núcleo irreducible'
of national character, one has a firm standpoint from
which to see the different manifestations of the country's
civilization in their true perspective and thence from
which to judge them. If they are found to be in harmony
with the national character they will be considered good;
if they are found to be out of harmony with that character
they will be considered bad:

> lo esencial en la Historia es el ligamen de los hechos con el
> espíritu del país donde han tenido lugar; solo a este precio
> se puede escribir una historia verdadera, lógica y útil. ¿A
> qué puede conducir una serie de hechos exactos y apoyados
> en pruebas fehacientes si se da a todos estos hechos igual
> valor, si se los presenta con el mismo relieve y no se marca
> cuáles son concordantes con el carácter de la nación, cuáles
> son opuestos, cuáles son favorables y cuáles contrarios a la
> evolución natural de cada territorio, considerado con sus
> habitantes como una personalidad histórica? (224)

Ganivet's criticism of the policy of Philip II is a good example of this thought in action: Philip II was a Spaniard who
inherited and sought to perpetuate a non-Spanish policy,
and the outcome, inevitably, was disastrous for the nation:

> Felipe II era un español y lo veía todo con ojos de español,
> con independencia y exclusivismo; así, no podía contentarse
> con la apariencia del poder; quería la realidad del poder
> [. . .]. La política de Felipe II tuvo el mérito que tiene todo
> lo que es franco y lógico: sirvió para deslindar los campos y
> para hacernos ver la gravedad de la empresa acometida por
> España al abandonar los cauces de su política nacional. Si
> Felipe II no triunfó por completo y dejó como herencia una

catástrofe inevitable, la culpa no fue suya, sino de la im-
posibilidad de amoldarse él y su nación a la táctica que
exigía y exige la política del continente (229-30).

en esta política [that of Philip II] había un error capital: el de
haber dirigido la acción de nuestro país por caminos ajenos
a nuestros intereses [. . .]. Todos estos desastres [deca-
dence, Peninsular disunity, the humiliation of Gibraltar, the
threatened loss of Spanish independence] vinieron eslabona-
dos y tuvieron su origen en la obcecación con que pretendi-
mos apoyarnos sobre ideas que carecían de asiento natural
en intereses reales (259-60).

But national character is not only a sound basis for a
proper judgement of the past; it is also the necessary basis
for a valid appreciation of the present and for an adequate
choice of policy for the future:

hay que tener una organización, y para que esta no sea de
puro artificio, para que cuaje y se afirme, ha de acomodarse a
nuestra constitución natural [. . .]. Hay que prescindir de
organizaciones artificiales, imitadas de los triunfadores del
día o de la víspera, y atenerse a lo que las necesidades propias exigen, sin fijarse en lo que hagan los demás. La
imitación de lo extraño tiene que concretarse a los detalles, a
todo aquello que sea progreso efectivo y encaje bien dentro
de la concepción nacional (197-8).

As long as a nation's thought is inadequately defined,
Ganivet believes, its action will be weak, imprecise and
transitory. A society must know where its destiny lies and
hence also its interests, 'como [. . .] un individuo que en
un momento cualquiera, recordando su pasado y exami-
nando su situación presente, se da cuenta precisa de lo
que es o lo que representa' (293). This, then, is the task of
the true politician: to know reality, especially the funda-

mental, ever-present, insistent reality of the national
spirit, to accept it, and to work consciously for its ful-
filment:

> Este es el único medio que tiene el hombre de influir prove-
> chosamente en el desarrollo de los sucesos históricos: cono-
> ciendo la realidad y sometiéndose a ella, no pretendiendo
> trastrocarla ni burlarla (243).

As in an individual so also in a nation self-knowledge is a
source of strength and ignorance of self is the path to
weakness. Again we can take an example from Ganivet's
study of Spain. 'What type of army organization should
Spain have?' he asks. For an answer he refers back to the
nation's alleged territorial spirit of independence:

> Véase, pues, cómo una idea que parece vaga e inaprisiona-
> ble, como la del espíritu del territorio, lleva en sí la solu-
> ción de grandes problemas políticos. Nosotros queremos
> tener ejércitos iguales a los del continente, y nuestro carácter
> pide, exige, un ejército peninsular. El soldado continental
> comprende la solidaridad y se siente más valiente y animoso
> cuando sabe que con él van contra el enemigo uno o dos
> millones, si es posible, de compañeros de armas. El soldado
> peninsular se encoge y se aflige y como que se ahoga cuando
> se ve anulado en una gran masa de tropas, porque adivina
> que no va a obrar allí humanamente, sino como un apa-
> rato mecánico. El número da al uno fuerzas y al otro se las
> quita [. . .].
> El mejor ejército español no será aquel que cuente con
> muchos soldados, sometidos a una sola cabeza, sino aquel
> que se componga de compañías que se muevan como un
> solo hombre y que tengan, como el dios Jano, dos caras:
> una mirando al campo, donde se libran las batallas regulares,
> y otra a la montaña, donde se encuentra un último y seguro
> refugio para defender la independencia nacional (196-9).

Ganivet makes such recommendations in the *Idearium* because he believes that Spain has abandoned her proper path. But behind this abandonment, far more grave than the abandonment itself, he finds a profound national incapacity for seeing where that true path lies. He attributes it to mental illness.

THE MALADY OF SPAIN: DIAGNOSIS AND PRESCRIPTION

At the root of the Spanish dilemma, says Ganivet, there is a serious mental illness: aboulia, 'extinción o debilitación grave de la voluntad' (286). In its more commonplace form, he affirms, we are all familiar with this malady as a state of mental perplexity in which the will is irresolute and inoperative because of the absence of any adequate guiding idea. In more serious cases the will stagnates in its repugnance for action and free acts are rarely carried to their conclusion, though instinctive acts are performed in the normal way. On the intellectual plane particular repugnance is felt for new ideas, but if a new idea does penetrate, it is not balanced by others and it reveals itself in exaltation and violence (286–7). Such is the malady of Spain. Whilst the routine acts of social life are performed instinctively, those that require the conscious intervention of the will are left undone, except that an idea will occasionally be seized upon with violence, out of its proper context:

> Nuestra nación hace ya tiempo que está como distraída en medio del mundo. Nada le interesa, nada le mueve de ordinario; mas de repente, una idea se fija, y, no pudiendo equilibrarse con otras, produce la impulsión arrebatada [. . .]. Todas nuestras obras intelectuales se resienten de esta

falta de equilibrio, de este error óptico; no vemos simultáneamente las cosas como son, puestas en sus lugares
respectivos, sino que las vemos a retazos, hoy unas, mañana
otras; la que un día estaba en primer término ocultando las
demás, al siguiente queda olvidada porque viene otra y se le
pone delante (289).

The cause of this aboulia, says Ganivet after considering various clinical interpretations, is 'la debilitación
del sentido sintético, de la facultad de asociar las representaciones' (291). The intelligence of the aboulic
functions normally when he is operating with established
ideas, but he is incapable of absorbing new ideas, incapable of associating them into the personal pattern of
his existing ideas. He lacks the necessary 'ideas céntricas'
around which intellectual data must be grouped. Hence
the extremes of his reaction to ideas, now violently
affirmative, now irresolute and impotent. Again Ganivet
seeks to apply his findings to the field of national psychology:

Y en tanto que el pensamiento de una nación no está claramente definido, la acción tiene que ser débil, indecisa, transitoria. El sentido sintético es en la sociedad, y en particular
en quienes la dirigen, la capacidad para obrar consciente-
mente, para conocer bien sus propios destinos (292–3).

It is a matter of understanding one's interests, of recalling
one's past and examining one's present situation. Some
nations, England for example (226, 238–9), are admirable
at this; others (and he is of course referring primarily to
Spain) are divided by individual interests and are therefore weak and unbalanced in their national actions:

Unas veces el móvil será la tradición, que jamás puede producir, aunque otra cosa se crea, un impulso enérgico, porque
en la vida intelectual lo pasado, así como es centro poderoso

> de resistencia, es principio débil de actividad; otras veces se
> obedecerá a una fuerza extraña, pues las sociedades débiles,
> como los artistas de pobre ingenio, suplen con las imita-
> ciones la falta de propia inspiración (293).

What is always lacking in these latter nations is 'la idea
clara, precisa, del interés común y de la acción constante,
serena, que se encamina a realizarlo' (294). Ganivet's
guiding aim in *Idearium español* is to fill this gap: to point
out the fundamental national interest of Spain and thereby to urge upon his readers the 'acción constante, serena,
que se encamina a realizarlo'.

But how is Ganivet to determine Spain's national interest? The method has already been suggested in his
diagnosis of the malady. Without the ability to synthesize,
he has said, intellectual efforts are useless and even harmful; in order to be profitable, intellectual data must be
gathered together around central ideas, 'ideas céntricas',
and new ideas must be accepted or rejected on the basis of
an established system. Similarly, in the field of civilization
thought and action must be in harmony with the 'fuerzas
constituyentes del alma de[l] país' (209):

> conforme transcurre el tiempo, se va notando que todas las
> funciones se rigen por una fuerza dominante y céntrica,
> donde pudiera decirse que está alojado el ideal de cada raza;
> y entonces comienza a distinguirse el carácter de las naciones
> y el papel que han representado con más perfección en la
> Historia o comedia universal (211).

Ganivet seeks to determine the 'fuerza dominante y
céntrica' of Spanish civilization in the belief that the
country's national interests will be served only by developments that are in harmony with that insistent, all-
pervading, dominant force.

Is he, then, simply a traditionalist seeking to justify his attachment to the past? An earlier quotation in this section suggests that he is not. A society that lacks the necessary faculty for synthesis, he has said, will be led at times by tradition and at other times by some outside force, but tradition can never produce an energetic impulse and submission to an outside influence is an acknowledgement of one's own debility (293). Pages before he made a similar point in his contrast between 'exclusivist (that is, traditional) education' and 'free education' (that is, education strongly influenced from abroad). Each one has its good side and each its bad:

La enseñanza exclusivista sería buena si los principios en que se inspira tuviesen vigor bastante, sin necesidad de las excitaciones de la controversia, para mantener vivas y fecundas las ciencias y las artes de la nación; por este sistema tendríamos una cultura un tanto estrecha de criterio e incompleta; pero, en cambio, tendríamos la unidad de inteligencia y de acción. Solo cuando las doctrinas decaen y pierden su fuerza creadora se hace necesario introducir levadura fresca que las haga de nuevo fermentar. La enseñanza libre—y no hablo de las formas ridículas que en la práctica ha tomado en España—tiene también, como todas las cosas, dos asas por donde cogerla: el punto flaco es la falta de congruencia entre las diferentes doctrinas, el desequilibrio intelectual que las ideas contradictorias suelen producir en las cabezas poco fuertes; la parte buena es la impulsión que se da al espíritu para que con absoluta independencia elija un rumbo propio y se eleve a concepciones originales (284-5).

Traditional education, says Ganivet, maintains the necessary national unity of thought and action but it is narrow and it lacks drive; foreign influenced education,

on the other hand, gives the impulse of free choice and
original thought, but it encourages the intellectual im-
balance that the author deplores. It is a problem that he
had already written about at length in his first doctorate
thesis, *España filosófica contemporánea*, but that work ended
on the threshold of conflict, with opposing systems placed
face to face and with Ganivet unable to see any means of
reconciling them. Now, in *Idearium español*, he has arrived
at his notion of Spanish national character and, both in
his judgement of the Spanish tradition and in his consideration of European influences, he emphasizes that
national character as a guide to what is appropriate to
Spain and hence also to what is desirable.

As an example of Ganivet's use of national character to
distinguish between the good and the bad within the
Spanish tradition we have seen his criticism of the foreign
policy of Philip II. 'Con Felipe II desaparece de nuestra
nación el sentido sintético' (231). The national spirit of
independence had been suppressed and the country was
no longer acting in accordance with its true native being.
Consequently men lacked the guidance of those all-
important 'ideas céntricas' of national character and they
ceased to see the national interests in their proper perspective, 'poniéndolo todo al mismo nivel: lo pasajero y
fugaz de nuestra política como lo esencial y permanente'
(231). It is the great error that underlies Spain's present
decadence also, says Ganivet, and the error causes even
greater sadness than the decadence, for among Spain's
political leaders 'no encontraremos uno solo que vea y
juzgue la política nacional desde un punto de vista elevado,
o, por lo menos, céntrico' (231-2).

As national character serves as a standpoint from which
to judge the Spanish tradition, so also it serves as a stand-

point from which to judge the relevance of foreign ideas
to Spanish civilization and as the necessary basis upon
which to Hispanize them:

> La imitación de lo extraño tiene que concretarse a los de-
> talles, a todo aquello que sea progreso efectivo y encaje bien
> dentro de la concepción nacional, pues a veces lo que en otro
> país es cuestión de primer orden, en el nuestro es menos que
> de segundo o tercero, y lo que es útil, inútil y hasta perjudi-
> cial, por falta de concord[anc]ia con lo esencial de nuestra
> organización (198).

> podremos recibir influencias extrañas, orientarnos estudian-
> do lo que hacen y dicen otras naciones; pero mientras no
> españolicemos nuestra obra, mientras lo extraño no esté
> sometido a lo español y vivamos en la incertidumbre en que
> hoy vivimos, no levantaremos cabeza (267).

Should Spain live as she has done up to the present, he
asks, or should she make a clean break with her bad traditions and become a well ordered 'nación a la moderna'
(197)? 'Ni esto, ni aquello [. . .]; hay que tener una
organización, y para que ésta no sea de puro artificio, para
que cuaje y se afirme, ha de acomodarse a nuestra constitución natural' (197). It would be artificial, Ganivet
insists, to cut the nation off from its tradition and launch
it upon a totally new existence 'como si fuéramos un
pueblo nuevo, acabado de sacar del horno' (281). On the
other hand, Spain is part of the modern world and must
also take account of modern ideas which, even if un-
acceptable in Spain, will at least serve to stimulate awareness of the nation's proper tradition, in the same way that
elements of religious dissidence would make Spaniards
more fully aware of their own deeply rooted Catholicism
(170-3). When national doctrines have lost their own

creative force, fresh yeast is required to make them ferment again (284).

In short, the essential Spanish tradition, that imposed by 'the essence of our territory' (236), and the European present must be reconciled:

> lo que nosotros debemos tomar de la tradición es lo que ella nos da o nos impone: el espíritu (272–3).

> no hay que romper la máquina [i.e. existing institutions]; lo que hay que hacer es echarle ideas, para que no ande en seco (285–6).[1]

Foreign influences are permissible and even desirable, but we should not seek to import ready-made solutions to our own national problems. The work of Spanish regeneration belongs to Spaniards alone (267). Foreign influences must be Hispanized; Spanish thought and action must be based on Spanish tradition:

> Cuanto en España se construya con carácter nacional debe estar sustentado sobre los sillares de la tradición (172).

THE MALADY OF SPAIN: CONVALESCENCE AND FUTURE MISSION

A country, says Ganivet, like an individual, prospers in so far as it remains true to its own native character; in so far as it acts against that character it weakens itself. Spain's native character, 'el espíritu permanente, invariable, que el territorio crea, infunde, mantiene en nosotros' (176), is a peninsular character of independence and this must be the basis for all adequate Spanish

---

[1] Cf. Todo cuanto viene de fuera a un país ha de acomodarse al espíritu del territorio si quiere ejercer una influencia real (*El porvenir de España*; II, 1064).

political action. But Spain has clearly abandoned her proper course: 'Apenas constituida la nación, nuestro espíritu se sale del cauce que le estaba marcado y se derrama por todo el mundo en busca de glorias exteriores y vanas' (219). Rivalry between different parts of the Peninsula at the time of the Reconquest caused a transformation of the spirit of independence into a spirit of conquest, and the energies accumulated during the eight centuries of the Reconquest were diverted to the New World instead of being concentrated within the Peninsula itself as a means of material restoration and a source of spiritual greatness. Then came Charles I, a continental by birth, who projected upon Spain his own continental ambitions and thereby completed the country's deviation from its natural course. Disaster was inevitable:

> Al empeñarse España, nación peninsular, en proceder como las naciones continentales, se condenaba a una ruina cierta, puesto que, si una nación se fortifica adquiriendo nuevos territorios que están dentro de su esfera de acción natural, se debilita en cambio con la agregación de otros que llevan consigo contingencias desfavorables a sus intereses propios y permanentes (226).

Philip II succeeded to the Habsburg policy, but Philip II was a Spaniard and he was therefore incapable of directing a continental policy. But he was also reluctant to abandon it. It is the point at which the Spanish national sense of synthesis broke down. Men had lost contact with the territorial spirit and thus with the necessary guiding force upon which their national thoughts and plans and actions should have been primarily based. They no longer saw things in perspective; psychologically they lacked the necessary 'ideas céntricas'; they placed everything on the same level of importance, 'lo pasajero y fugaz de nuestra política como lo esencial y permanente' (231). They had no basis upon which to distinguish the good from the bad within the Spanish tradition and they had no means of judging the adequacy or inadequacy of influences received from abroad. The result was the state of aboulia in which Spain still lives on today, a state of political and spiritual prostration disrupted by periodic outbursts of violence as one idea or another is seized upon, out of its proper context, as an incentive to action. In the following passage Ganivet sums up his findings on the situation of Spain at the moment of writing and prepares the way for his own recommendations for a more adequate national policy:

> La fábrica española ha estado parada durante largos años por falta de motor; hoy empieza a moverse porque hemos aligerado, o nos han aligerado, el artefacto, y ya hay quien desea volver a las antiguas complicaciones, en vez de trabajar por aumentar la escasa fuerza motriz de que hoy disponemos. De aquí la necesidad perentoria de destruir las ilusiones nacionales; y el destruirlas no es obra de desesperados: es obra de noble y legítima ambición, por la cual comenzamos a fundar nuestro positivo engrandecimiento (271).

Those who would have the country return to its 'antiguas complicaciones' are the jingoistic imperialists who think only of blood-spilling and who seek to embroil the country again in foreign escapades alien to its true character (221). Ganivet had already attacked them in his *Epistolario* (II, 915–19). Illusions of conquest by force of arms must be destroyed, he says; blood-spilling is not enough in civilized peoples: 'hay que luchar por el engrandecimiento ideal de la gran familia en medio de la cual se ha nacido, y este engrandecimiento exige algo más que el mero sacrificio de la vida' (222).

The necessary preliminary to 'engrandecimiento ideal' is 'restauración material': 'trabajar por aumentar la escasa fuerza motriz de que hoy disponemos'. Ganivet makes no recommendations for economic reform, though he does refer—without further definition—to the need for 'una restauración política y social de un orden completamente nuevo' (280). In general, he appears to believe that there is sufficient energy generated within the Peninsula, if only this energy is not squandered on foreign adventures:

Una restauración de la vida entera de España no puede tener otro punto de arranque que la concentración de todas nuestras energías dentro de nuestro territorio. Hay que cerrar con cerrojos, llaves y candados todas las puertas por donde el espíritu español se escapó de España para derramarse por los cuatro puntos del horizonte, y por donde hoy espera que ha de venir la salvación; y en cada una de esas puertas no pondremos un rótulo dantesco que diga: 'Lasciate ogni speranza', sino este otro más consolador, más humano, muy profundamente humano, imitado de San Agustín: 'Noli foras ire; in interiore Hispaniae habitat veritas' (276-7).[1]

[1] This passage is too often quoted, without qualification, as evidence of Ganivet's inward-looking traditionalism and of his desire to isolate Spain from all outside influences. It must, of course, be considered in its proper context and be weighed against his clear statements elsewhere about the desirability and even the necessity of foreign influences (see above, 'The Approach to Spain' and 'The Malady of Spain: Diagnosis and Prescription'). His main purpose in recommending 'locked gates' is to prevent the escape of national energies. For the rest, he is surely objecting here only to the importation of ready-made solutions that are not rooted in Spanish character and thus are not appropriate to the Spanish situation (see especially 267). The adaptation from Saint Augustine, the original of which Ganivet may well have recalled from his school textbook of psychology (MLA, pp. 52-3), would then not give a completely true notion of Ganivet's thought. For it is not truth that resides in Spain (Does not Ganivet in any case object to such absolutes? 165-70). What

nuestras aspiraciones de puertas afuera o son infundadas o utópicas, o realizables a tan largo plazo que no es posible distraer a causa de ellas la atención y continuar viviendo a la expectativa. La única indicación eficaz que del examen de nuestros intereses exteriores se desprende es que debemos robustecer la organización que hoy tenemos y adquirir una fuerza intelectual muy intensa, porque nuestro papel histórico nos obliga a transformar nuestra acción de material en espiritual (280).

So far, then, Ganivet has decried the errors of Spanish policy since the end of the Reconquest and especially since the coming of the Habsburgs. He has sought to show how, since then, the fundamental character of the nation has been suppressed and the country itself been weakened. Finally, he has advocated a policy of 're-traimiento voluntario' (235), with the renunciation of material commitments abroad and the concentration of

resides in Spain is the necessary basis for arriving at a totally adequate national policy (that is, the means of arriving at a relative truth), 'el cimiento sobre el que se debe construir' (167) and to which foreign influences must be subordinated and adapted. Nevertheless, against this argument it might be objected that Ganivet also says elsewhere that Spain must forge a completely new political and social order and that 'ni las ideas francesas, ni las inglesas, ni las alemanas, ni las que puedan más tarde estar en boga, nos sirven' (281). This is one of the difficulties of presenting a simple exposition of Ganivet's ideas: his laxity of thought and expression frequently gives rise to inconsistencies. Even in the lines just referred to, a more obvious example of inconsistency presses itself upon us. Spain, he has said, must work for 'una restauración política y social de un orden completamente nuevo' (280). How is this to be reconciled with the recommendation, also quoted in the text above— and more generally characteristic of Ganivet's thought—, 'que debemos robustecer la organización que hoy tenemos' (280)? But I shall be pointing to far more serious discrepancies than these in later chapters. For the moment, I may be permitted to anticipate one of my later findings and point out that Ganivet's thought in *Idearium español* is itself strongly influenced by foreign ideas, though he adapts these to the Spanish situation. Consequently, if his recommendations for Spain's future were put into practice, the Spanish nation would certainly have undergone outside influences—as Ganivet is wont to allow and to recommend.

national energies within the country itself as is demanded
by the territorial spirit of independence. By this means, he
believes, Spain will be spiritually regenerated and he
declares this to be the 'motivo céntrico' of his ideas (295).
Essentially, such regeneration will be the work of individuals, intelligent, unprejudiced individuals, 'hombres
poseídos por el patriotismo silencioso' (296), but individual efforts must not be allowed to become the basis
for impetuous action, and intellectual conflicts must not
give rise to real-life conflicts. An idea becomes a useful
force in a nation only when it accepts and adapts itself to
that nation's 'intellectual solidarity' (298). At the centre of
that solidarity is the mysterious force [presumably the
spirit of independence] that has been so neglected and
stifled during recent centuries of Spanish history. And so
Ganivet arrives at his national credo:

> Yo tengo fe en el porvenir espiritual de España; en esto soy
> acaso exageradamente optimista. Nuestro engrandecimiento
> material nunca nos llevaría a oscurecer el pasado; nuestro
> florecimiento intelectual convertirá el siglo de oro de nues-
> tras artes en una simple anunciación de este siglo de oro que
> yo confío ha de venir. Porque en nuestros trabajos ten-
> dremos de nuestra parte una fuerza desconocida, que vive
> en estado latente en nuestra nación, al modo que en el
> símil con que comencé este libro vivían en el alma de la
> mujer casada contra su gusto y madre fecundísima contra
> su deseo los nobles y puros y castos sentimientos de la vir-
> ginidad. Esa fuerza misteriosa está en nosotros, y aunque
> hasta ahora no se ha dejado ver, nos acompaña y nos vigila;
> hoy es acción desconcertada y débil, mañana será calor y
> luz y hasta, si se quiere, electricidad y magnetismo (300).[1]

[1] Cf. Yo rechazo todo lo que sea sumisión, y tengo fe en la virtud creadora de nuestra tierra. Mas para crear es necesario que la nación, como
el hombre, se recojan y mediten, y España ha de reconcentrar todas

Because of long contact with the Arabs, Spain has the Semitic element that characterized both Greek civilization and Christianity, the 'fuego ideal' that the Indo-Europeans themselves lack:

> En general, puede establecerse como ley histórica que, dondequiera que la raza indoeuropea se pone en contacto con la semítica, surge un nuevo y vigoroso renacimiento ideal [. . .]. Así, pues, los que con desprecio y encono sistemáticos descartan de nuestra evolución espiritual la influencia arábiga, cometen un crimen psicológico y se incapacitan para comprender el carácter español (302).

The potentiality of Spanish 'ideal' greatness is thus assured. The Spanish Renaissance was stunted through the deviation of Spanish history from its proper course. But the essential native character still lives on today, and it is that character that must be accepted as the basis of Spain's future greatness.

> esa fuerza que hoy es un obstáculo para la vida regular de la nación, porque se la aplica a lo que no debe aplicársela, ha de sufrir un desdoblamiento; el individualismo indisciplinado que hoy nos debilita y nos impide levantar cabeza, ha de ser algún día individualismo interno y creador y ha de conducirnos a nuestro gran triunfo ideal. Tenemos lo principal: el hombre, el tipo; nos falta solo decidirle a que ponga manos en la obra [. . .].
>
> Así como creo que para las aventuras de la dominación material muchos pueblos de Europa son superiores a nosotros, creo también que para la creación ideal no hay ninguno con aptitudes naturales tan depuradas como las nuestras (303-4).

---

sus fuerzas y abandonar el campo de la lucha estéril, en el que hoy combate por un imposible, con armas compradas al enemigo (*El provenir de España*; II, 1073).

But Spain's spiritual regeneration is not proposed by Ganivet simply as an end in itself. His country, he believes, has a great historical mission: to guide the Hispanic peoples of the world. At present, he says, because of her state of exhaustion, Spain is unfit for such a role. Material and spiritual restoration are necessary before the nation can fulfil its destiny:

> Necesitamos reconstituir nuestras fuerzas materiales para resolver nuestros asuntos interiores, y nuestra fuerza ideal para influir en la esfera de nuestros legítimos intereses externos, para fortificar nuestro prestigio en los pueblos de origen hispánico (266–7).

But is not Spain a peninsular nation unsuited to such imperial exploits? Had she not already been expelled from most of her American possessions? By what means and in what manner is she to re-establish herself as the principal guide of Hispanic destinies? For an answer to these questions we must consider Ganivet's treatment of Spanish colonization in America (especially, 244–56).

Ganivet accepts as his starting-point the notable contrasts between the effects of English colonization in North America and the effects of Spanish colonization in Central and South America. On the one hand, he finds the powerful, wealthy and apparently well-governed United States, which presumes to exert its protection over the whole American continent and whose political institutions have been seized upon by some European statesmen as their model; on the other hand, he finds poor, badly governed countries torn by civil wars and *pronunciamientos* and ridden by the worst sort of militarism. The fact is, says Ganivet, that Spain has imprinted upon Latin America her own territorial spirit of independence—witness the

variety of the different Latin American republics—, and
because of that spirit of independence Latin American
countries have refused to import ready-made solutions
from the mother country. Unlike the United States, they
have preferred to start again with the uncertainties and the
stumblings of their own infancy. It is a sign of vitality,
Ganivet maintains, from which real progress will follow,
but it means also that Latin American Spaniards are
suspicious of the metropolis and react against all Spanish
attempts at material intervention in their affairs. This
prompts Ganivet to oppose the idea of any type of Ibero-
American union. 'En nuestra raza,' he affirms, 'no hay
peor medio para lograr la unión que proponérselo y
anunciarlo con [ruido y con] aparato' (248). Spanish influence must be exerted more discreetly, by means of
intellectual bonds which are too subtle to provoke
opposition. Hence his proposal for a 'Confederación
intelectual o espiritual'. This requires, firstly, that Spain
should possess adequate ideas, and secondly, that she
should give those ideas freely to facilitate their propagation. For in Spanish-speaking countries, Ganivet emphasizes, Spain has a duty: 'el deber de luchar para que
nuestra tradición no se extinga, para conservar la unidad y
la pureza del lenguaje' (251). Spain must re-establish her
intellectual prestige; she must make herself the spiritual
guide of Spanish America. Spain and the Latin American
countries are blood brothers:

> si por el solo esfuerzo de nuestra inteligencia lográsemos
> reconstituir la unión familiar de todos los pueblos hispánicos
> e infundir en ellos el culto de unos mismos ideales, de
> nuestros ideales, cumpliríamos una gran misión histórica y
> daríamos vida a una creación grande, original, nueva en los
> fastos políticos (282).

But there are several doubtful points here in Ganivet's argument and one of them is so fundamental that mention of it can hardly be avoided in the context of this chapter. How can the policy that Ganivet advocates be reconciled with the Spanish spirit of independence—that is, of non-involvement—on which he has insisted so much? Can material domination in Latin America be so completely separated from intellectual domination (where the *'lazos de subordinación* que esta crea' are more subtle, 248; my italics) that the one is opposed to Spain's spirit of independence and the other one in harmony with it? Besides, if Ganivet's insistence on the territorial spirit is justified, should Latin American countries not be left, now, to adapt themselves gradually to their own newly acquired continental geology? And apart from any territorial spirit, are there not now considerable differences between Spain and Latin America?[1] And to employ for a moment Ganivet's own imagery (252), has one member of a 'family' the right to press his domination on his 'brothers', even if it is only intellectual domination? Unamuno's observation is surely relevant:

El único modo de elevar al prójimo es ayudarle a que sea más *él* cada vez, a que se depure en su línea propia, no en la nuestra (*El porvenir de España; OC* IV, 1958, 963).[2]

[1] The Colombian writer, Baldomero Sanín Cano, has emphasized such differences in his book *El humanismo y el progreso del hombre*, Buenos Aires 1955, pp. 220–58.
[2] One may recall also the following passage by Ganivet himself:
Yo encuentro a un hombre caído en medio de la calle, y le ayudo a ponerse en pie, y después le dejo ir sin preguntarle adónde va. ¿Sería justo que por haberle levantado le obligase a venirse conmigo? Pues esto hacen los hombres, todos los hombres, cuando prestan un servicio intelectual, lo prestan para que el discípulo se someta a las ideas del maestro (*Los trabajos de Pío Cid*; II, 222).

Finally, if Hispanic peoples *are* to be united by common ideals, with what justification can Ganivet assume that these 'mismos ideales' should be 'nuestros [i.e. Spanish] ideales' (282)?

All these questions become especially urgent when one considers the following rather negative reasons for imposing Spanish ideas:

Dejemos a otros pueblos practicar la colonización utilitaria y continuemos nosotros con nuestro sistema tradicional, *que, malo o bueno, es al fin nuestro.* Estamos ya demasiado avanzados para cambiar de rumbo, y aunque quisiéramos no podríamos tomar otro nuevo, y aunque pudiéramos no adelantaríamos nada con superponer a un edificio construido con arreglo a nuestras ideas un cuerpo más de estilo diferente, copiado quizá sin discernimiento. No hemos podido formar un concepto propio sobre la colonización a la moderna; atengámonos al antiguo, prosigámoslo con tenacidad, aunque choque con las ideas corrientes; *porque si nosotros no tenemos fe en las obras que creamos, ¿quién la tendrá por nosotros y cuál será nuestra misión en la historia futura?* (267–8; my italics)

If Spanish ideas are of doubtful validity to the modern situation, as Ganivet here appears to suggest, might it not be more noble to invoke the spirit of independence entirely and recommend that Spanish energies should be contained *completely* within Spanish frontiers? The country's great age of imperial adventure would then be quite finished and Spain would have found true national independence.

In short, if we accept the territorial spirit of independence as the all-important factor in the Spanish national constitution and, with it, the determinism that underlies Ganivet's reasoning, the conclusion is inevitable: Spain should withdraw from all involvements outside her own frontiers. But the spirit of independence is not the only element emphasized by Ganivet in the Spanish con-stitution—or in his treatment of Spanish colonization:

> Los descubrimientos y conquistas en América, que tan profunda brecha nos abrieron, tenían también su justi-ficación en nuestro carácter, en nuestra fe y en la fatalidad providencial con que nos cayó sobre los hombros tan pesada carga (226).

Spain's intervention in European continental affairs was 'un inconmensurable absurdo político' (226), but her action in America was partly justified, Ganivet believes, by the nation's militant Catholicism and he does not wholly condemn the venture.[1] Moreover, there was a time, he says, at the end of the Reconquest, when Spanish intervention in Africa would have been both justified and destined to succeed 'tanto porque nacía lógicamente de nuestra historia medieval, cuanto porque no hubiera chocado con los intereses de Europa' (275). The latter reason is purely negative, and at the centre of the former is, once again, the Spanish religious spirit, forged during the Reconquest (160–2). Finally, Spain is not at present called to intervene in the Mediterranean, says Ganivet, but if she does have to intervene it must be 'con su carácter de nación católica' (260). For Ganivet, then, Spanish religious faith is, within the national constitution, the one important element that justifies departures from the demands of the territorial spirit of independence, and

---

[1] Cf. España fue [a América] animada por un ideal. Durante la Re-conquista se formó en España ese ideal, fundiéndose las aspiraciones del Estado y la Iglesia y tomando cuerpo la fe en la vida política. *La fe activa, militante, conquistadora, fue nuestro móvil*, la cual creó en breve sus propios instrumentos de acción: ejércitos y armadas, grandes políticos y diplomáticos (*El porvenir de España*; II, 1093; my italics).

it is that faith especially that justifies and will be at the centre of the spiritual guidance that Spain is urged to offer Hispanic peoples everywhere. The religious note in the final paragraph of the book is surely significant.

But in these last pages I have strayed from my declared path of simple exposition. I have been incited to ask questions. It has become difficult to withhold criticisms. I pass, then, to the main part of my study and begin by developing the duality that has just been uncovered in the author's treatment of Spain's mission.

III

STOICISM AND THE SPIRIT
OF INDEPENDENCE

According to Ganivet each country has its own psychological structure, and to understand that structure one
must probe beneath the external manifestations of civilization and discover the 'núcleo irreducible al que están
adheridas todas las envueltas' (175). This 'núcleo irreducible', he believes, is to be found in the territorial spirit,
'el espíritu permanente, invariable, que el territorio crea,
infunde, mantiene en nosotros' (176). Since Spain is a
peninsula, her insistent, all-pervading spirit is one of
independence.

But the territorial spirit of independence is not the only
'fuerza constituyente' of the Spanish soul. Another one is
emphasized strongly:

> Cuando se examina la constitución ideal de España, el
> elemento moral y en cierto modo religioso más profundo
> que en ella se descubre, como sirviéndole de cimiento, es el
> estoicismo (151).

Stoicism, like the territorial spirit of independence, reveals
itself as soon as one probes beneath the external manifestations of Spanish civilization, 'en cuanto se ahonda un poco
en la superficie o corteza ideal de nuestra nación' (152).
As with the territorial spirit of independence, too, the
hypothesis of stoicism (Ganivet would say the recognition
of stoicism) enables one to see elements of Spanish civilization in what the author believes to be their proper
perspective.

I shall examine Ganivet's case for each of these 'fuerzas constituyentes' in turn. I begin, as Ganivet himself begins, with stoicism.

STOICISM

Let us observe immediately that Ganivet offers little factual evidence for his case. He begins by affirming the fundamental importance of stoicism in Spain's 'ideal constitution' and thereafter seeks to justify his claim by showing its effectiveness as an explanation of Spain's moral and religious evolution since pre-Christian times. In fact, he does not make a very convincing case. Instead, he guides his reader through a maze of argument in which he appears to disprove his own initial claim.

To justify this criticism it is necessary to recall the steps in Ganivet's argument. And first, his initial claim:

> Cuando se examina la constitución ideal de España, el elemento moral y en cierto modo religioso más profundo que en ella se descubre, como sirviéndole de cimiento, es el estoicismo [. . .]. Es inmensa, mejor dicho, inmensurable, la parte que al senequismo toca en la conformación religiosa, y moral, y aun en el derecho consuetudinario de España; en el arte y en la ciencia vulgar, en los proverbios, máximas y refranes, y aun en aquellas ramas de la ciencia culta en que Séneca no paró mientes jamás (151-3).

Stoicism, Ganivet claims, is a fundamental characteristic of the Spaniard, 'y es tan español que Séneca no tuvo que inventarlo, porque lo encontró inventado ya' (152). Here, of course, he apparently overlooks the fact that Seneca was taken to Rome as a baby and remained there for the rest of his life. But perhaps, with the words 'lo encontró inventado ya', Ganivet means that Seneca inherited stoicism from his parents as an element of race rather than that he discovered it around him as an element of national environment. It is a minor point that one need not press; Ganivet is not very critical in his use of language.

Far more serious is the violent turn that his reasoning takes almost immediately afterwards (154–7). His argument, if I understand it correctly (for I do not, like Ganivet, find it 'patente e innegable'), consists of two premisses and a conclusion. His first premiss is this: that stoicism was the natural response, at a particular moment in time, to the exhaustion of Graeco-Roman philosophy, but that because of its lack of positive goals it prepared the way for men's subsequent acceptance of a faith. His second premiss is similar but takes its starting point in a different field: Christian morality, he alleges, with its initial condemnation of action was the natural response, at a particular moment in time, to the exhaustion of Hebrew theology, but because of its lack of positive goals it prepared the way for the acceptance of reason. From this juxtaposition of doubtful premisses Ganivet concludes that stoicism therefore prepared the way for a new Christianity of purging fire, 'una creencia que penetrase, no en forma de símbolos, venidos a la sazón muy a menos, sino en forma de rayo ideal, taladrando e incendiando' (156). This, claims Ganivet, is what Christianity became in the vast areas that stoicism had made ready. Moreover, through stoicism Christianity inherited the tradition of pagan philosophy and Seneca is like a doctor of the Church.

Now if this is a fair summary of Ganivet's argument (and I believe it is), he would appear to have undermined his own initial claim that stoicism is a fundamental characteristic of the Spanish people. In the first place, he has brought together stoicism and Christianity in their 'relación patente e innegable' only by showing that stoicism was not a peculiarity of Spain but that it was common to all those parts of the world that inherited the Classical tradition; in the second place, he has brought stoicism and Christian morality together at a point in time as transitory solutions ('esa solución [el senequismo] es transitoria', 'esa moral [Christian morality in its initial phase] es transitoria'), and thereby, it would appear, denied their relevance to later periods of Spanish civilization. Christianity, of course, lived on, but in a different form, says Ganivet: as 'un fuego ardiente', 'en forma de rayo ideal'. And in Spain stoicism also lived on, he claims, and Seneca seems like a doctor of the Church. But Ganivet gives no evidence and I am unable to follow his reasoning. It is contained completely in the following lines:

> Mientras que aparentemente no se descubre más que una propagación, la del cristianismo, en secreto se efectuaba otra propagación, la de la filosofía gentílica, cristianizada; y el punto en que tuvo lugar la conjunción, el injerto, fue la moral estoica. Así en España, donde era el asiento del estoicismo más lógico, no del más perfecto, del más humano, el senequismo se mezcla con el Evangelio de tal suerte, que de nuestro Séneca, si no puede decirse en rigor que 'huele a santo', sí puede afirmarse que tiene todo el aire de un doctor de la Iglesia (157).[1]

One thing is certain—and we shall see this subsequently—: that after these initial pages stoicism plays very little part

---

[1] According to Unamuno, Ganivet was here misled by a purely external resemblance between Christianity and 'el pagano moralismo senequista' (*El porvenir de España*; *OC* IV, 1958, 963); according to Laín Entralgo, he was wrong to liken Seneca to a doctor of the Church (in *Ensayos y Estudios* II, 1940, 79).

in *Idearium español*. Where it does seem to appear, it can more accurately be called determinism. The one element from these introductory pages that does live on throughout the book is not stoicism but crusading fervour, the burning, purging, purifying Christianity whose way Ganivet believes to have been prepared by stoicism and which he finds to have been intensified in Spain by the Moslem occupation. We shall see shortly the enormous significance of this fact.

Before passing to the territorial spirit of independence, a last brief point must be made about the pages just discussed. Ganivet, I have suggested, is somewhat lax in his use of language and I have given an example. But it is not only laxity of language that disturbs us as we read the *Idearium*; it is also laxity of thought. There are several examples in his pages on stoicism and one of them is especially striking, for it is central to his argument: namely, the part that reason plays in stoicism. The following are the most significant lines:

> y entonces surge la moral estoica, moral sin base, fundada solo en la virtud o en la dignidad; pero esa solución es transitoria, porque bien pronto el hombre, menospreciando las fuerzas de su razón que no le conducen a nada positivo, cierra los ojos y acepta una creencia (154).

(Here Ganivet appears to see stoicism as characterized by the 'forces of reason'.)

> la moral estoica, fundada legítimamente sobre lo único que la filosofía había dejado en pie, sobre lo que subsiste aún en los periodos de mayor decadencia, el instinto de nuestra propia dignidad, era negativa tanto para griegos como para romanos, porque, derivada del esfuerzo racional, pretendía constituirlo todo sin el apoyo de la razón por un acto de

adhesión ciega, que andaba tan cerca de la fe como la moral
cristiana andaba cerca de la pura razón (155).

(Here Ganivet seems to find in stoicism a reaction against
reason.)

Lo noble, lo justo, lo humanitario [he is referring to stoic
morality again], sostenido y amparado solo por la razón,
menos que por la razón por el instinto, no puede ni podrá
jamás vencer las pasiones bajas, ruines y animales de la
generalidad de los hombres (155).

(Here Ganivet embraces both views of stoicism at once,
in a single mystifying juxtaposition.)

Is it through lack of intellectual discipline that Ganivet
shifts his position in this way, or is it that each presentation is the one best suited to that particular stage in his
argument? The first would certainly appear to be true; the
second also. We shall find further examples.

THE TERRITORIAL SPIRIT

The following lines present the nucleus of Ganivet's reflections on the subject:

Como hay continentes, penínsulas e islas, así hay también
espíritus continentales, peninsulares e insulares [. . .]: en los
pueblos continentales lo característico es la resistencia, en
los peninsulares la independencia, y en los insulares la
agresión. El principio general es el mismo, la conservación;
pero los continentales, que tienen entre sí relaciones fre-
cuentes y forzosas, la confían al espíritu de resistencia; los
peninsulares, que viven más aislados, aunque no libres de
ataques e invasiones, no necesitados de una organización
defensiva permanente, sino de unión en caso de peligro, la
confían al espíritu de independencia, que se exacerba con las

agresiones; los insulares que viven en territorio aislado, con límites fijos e invariables, menos expuestos, por tanto, a las invasiones, se ven impelidos, cuando les obliga a ello la necesidad de acción, a convertirse en agresores (176-7).

England is an example of the island spirit, France an example of the continental spirit, and Spain an example of the peninsular spirit. The distinction is appealing in its simplicity and the examples are admirably chosen: the history of England has in fact been a history of aggression, and the history of France has been largely a history of frontier wars, and the history of Spain . . . , but here Ganivet himself is pointing out a divergence from the country's proper path and it is central to his study.

And yet Ganivet's distinctions are not convincing and as a preliminary to disagreement with them it must be pointed out that the words *aggression*, *resistance* and *independence* are not mutually exclusive terms; they may simply express different view-points on a same action. A particular country seizes a piece of land. It is a clear act of aggression. But aggression is surely motivated. Perhaps it was to ensure trade routes, or to establish a safer frontier, or to uphold the right of one's royal cousin, the 'rightful heir' to a disputed throne. In each of these cases one can talk of *aggression*, but in each of these cases also one can talk of the need to ensure one's *independence* from outside pressures and the need to strengthen one's *resistance* to those pressures. Modern international propaganda has taught us much about the use of such words. The 're-sistance' bands who fought heroically for their 'indepen-dence' in one decade of Foreign Office reports may well be the 'aggressors' of the following decade. The intelli-gent observer of today is critical of such terms; Ganivet was not.

F

A single example will serve—of many possible ones.
Ganivet is emphasizing the Spanish spirit of independence
and contrasting it with the English spirit of aggression:

> Y en nuestra historia interior, siendo, como es por des-
> gracia, fertilísima en guerras civiles, no existen tampoco
> guerras de agresión, sino luchas por la independencia. La
> unión nace por la paz y en virtud de enlaces o del derecho
> hereditario; así se unieron Aragón y Cataluña, Castilla y
> Aragón, España y Portugal. La guerra aparece solo al
> separarse; de un lado se combate por la independencia; del
> otro por conservar la unidad; es decir, la legalidad política
> establecida; por tanto, no hay agresión. Un hecho como la
> ocupación de Gibraltar por Inglaterra, sin derecho ni pre-
> cedente que lo justifique, por cálculo y por conveniencia, no
> existe en nuestra historia (186–7).

But may not an alliance also be a form of aggression? If
it provokes struggles for independence it would appear
to be so. But here we have no need to make a case, for
elsewhere in the *Idearium* Ganivet makes it for us. He is
writing of the Catalan and Aragonese tendency to 'conquista apoyada por la política y la diplomacia' (184) and
he quotes Castelar with evident approval on the case of
Navarre:

> 'La incorporación de Navarra a la corona de España—ha
> dicho Castelar—es un capítulo de Maquiavelo.' (184)

What is here said of the incorporation of Navarre in 1512–
1515, may it not also be said of the incorporation of Portugal in 1580? And who would deny a considerable element
of physical aggression in Ferdinand the Catholic's invasion
of Navarre? Spanish aggression against Navarre, Spanish
resistance to France—the Navarrese episode can perhaps

as well be presented in these terms as it can in terms of the Spanish spirit of independence.

But let us not exaggerate. One does not always object to the emphasis Ganivet gives to a particular country's history by classifying it as aggressive or resistant or independent. Certainly he has some authority for considering English history to have been largely one of aggression. In the case of France, on the other hand, one thinks of François I and Richelieu and Mazarin and Louis XIV, and one is not convinced that the term 'resistant' is completely justified. Ganivet himself recognizes an even more obvious exception—that of Napoleon. But Napoleon was a foreigner and an islander, says Ganivet, and he behaved throughout with the aggression and the tactics of an islander (180). Here one must remind Ganivet of one of the basic tenets of determinist thought: that an individual, in public matters especially, thrives only in so far as he is in harmony with the national spirit, just as the country itself thrives only in so far as it is at one with its own fundamental character. Ganivet himself invokes this principle elsewhere in his book (with another shift of position to suit the argument of the moment):

> Si la idea de un gran estadista fuese arbitraria o caprichosa, ajena al pensamiento y al sentimiento generales, no podría adelantar un paso (292).

If the story of Napoleon's success represents an exception to this principle, we must surely expect Ganivet to give some explanation, which he does not do; if, on the other hand, it is the determinist assumption that is mistaken, then Ganivet's whole study falls down, for, as we shall see shortly, it is constructed upon that assumption. Moreover, if he fails to account for Napoleon, he fails also to account for the 'agresiones absurdas y contrarias a los intereses de Francia' of the Second Empire and the Third Republic, which he sees as attempts to continue Napoleon's policy (180).

Now let us turn to Spain. The spirit of Spain is a spirit of independence, her history 'una serie inacabable de invasiones y de expulsiones, una guerra permanente de independencia' (181). It is a tempting premiss. Much has been written about Spanish individualism, and the term 'guerra de independencia' strikes a familiar note. But on what does Ganivet establish his premiss? Simply on the following reasoning:

> los peninsulares, que viven más aislados, aunque no libres de ataques e invasiones, no necesitados de una organización defensiva permanente, sino de unión en caso de peligro, la confían al espíritu de independencia, que se exacerba con las agresiones [. . .]. El peninsular conoce asimismo cuál es el punto débil de su territorio, porque por él ha visto entrar siempre a los invasores; pero como su espíritu de resistencia y previsión no ha podido tomar cuerpo por falta de relaciones constantes con otras razas, se deja invadir fácilmente, lucha en su propia casa por su independencia, y, si es vencido, se amalgama con sus vencedores con mayor facilidad que los continentales [. . .]. En España, considerándonos casi aislados, por lo mismo que somos una casi isla, concentramos nuestro pensamiento en el punto por donde puede venir el ataque, y de esta concentración nace el sentimiento de independencia; somos casi independientes y queremos serlo del todo (177-9).

Surely this is inadequate. Could not an equally strong case have been made, with a slight difference of emphasis in the terms used, to show that a peninsular geology encourages a spirit of resistance or a spirit of aggression?

Besides, even if one allows Ganivet's premiss to be adequately founded, Spanish history denies the conditions that Ganivet demands for the formation of the territorial spirit of independence. These are the relevant lines:

> hay que ir más hondo y buscar en la realidad misma el núcleo irreducible al que están adheridas todas las envueltas que van transformando en el tiempo la fisonomía de ese país. Y, como siempre que se profundiza, se va a dar en lo único que hay para nosotros perenne, la tierra, ese núcleo se encuentra en el *espíritu territorial.* La religión, con ser algo muy hondo, no es lo más hondo que hay en una nación; la religión cambia, mientras que el espíritu territorial subsiste, porque los cambios geológicos vienen tan de tarde en tarde, que a veces nacen y mueren varias civilizaciones sin que el suelo ofrezca un cambio perceptible (175).

A territorial spirit demands vast periods of time for its formation, outstripping the life-span of religions. But for how long has it been possible for the peoples of the Iberian Peninsula to consider themselves as a peninsular unit, to have any awareness of belonging together in a peninsula? I am not referring to the difficulty of communications (though this may well be relevant); I am referring to the fact that until the fifteenth century Spain was composed of a number of separate, independent states, 'pequeños estados que andaban encerrados y alejados del campo de la lucha' (183) (I use Ganivet's own words, though he is of course here trying to prove a different point with them.) How would the position of Navarre up to and during the Middle Ages, for example, be different from that of Belgium or Switzerland today? If the presence of foreign powers around one's frontiers produces a continental spirit of resistance, should the spirit of Navarre not also be a spirit of resistance? And might not the same be said of other parts of the Peninsula, and of other parts of Europe that are now united in large national units? Is Ganivet not guilty of a serious anachronism in viewing whole geological immensities of time from the narrowness of our own few hundred years of modern history? The question becomes even more urgent when one considers that, during these few hundred years, Spain, by Ganivet's own admission, has not acted like a peninsular nation.

But here Ganivet himself sees the more obvious objection and he makes it the chief reason for his claim that Spain has abandoned her proper path:

> Si por naturaleza no somos agresivos, ¿cómo entender nuestra historia moderna, en la que España, apenas constituida, aparece como una nación guerrera y conquistadora? (181–2).

As in his treatment of Napoleon, Ganivet invokes special circumstances to explain this departure from the alleged territorial spirit: when Castile, because of its central position, assumed the principal role in the Reconquest and promised to become the predominant power, Portugal and Aragon sought to ensure their independence within the peninsula by strengthening themselves without, and Castile took over their aggressiveness out of a sense of rivalry and carried it to the four points of the compass. It was a deviation from the country's essential being, Ganivet believes, and it will inevitably disappear as the country returns to its proper course: that demanded by the peninsular spirit of independence. We shall pursue this argument later. For the moment we cannot do so because it becomes involved with the other allegedly principal 'fuerza constituyente' of the Spanish soul, stoicism and Christian fervour.

To sum up. Ganivet assumes three main types of territorial spirit according to the three main types of land formation and he proposes one main example of each. The examples are well chosen and it is difficult to think of any other three that would fit his case as well. Nevertheless, his case, I believe, is unsatisfactory. In the first place, there is a rather lax use of the terms *aggression, resistance* and *independence* that reduces the value of the distinction proposed. Thus, it is doubtful whether even English history can be regarded simply as aggressive, and in view of the special case that Ganivet makes for Portugal and Aragon, one is encouraged to suggest that perhaps England also was seeking to establish some kind of independence—or some kind of resistance—in her manifestly aggressive foreign policy. But Ganivet's case for England is strong. His case for France is less strong. Even before Napoleon one is not convinced that her foreign policy was only, or even principally, one of resistance, and the case of Napoleon is so clear that Ganivet himself is obliged to mention it, and to give a special, rather doubtful, explanation. His case for Spain is still less strong. His notion of a fundamental national spirit of independence is backed up by no adequate evidence and most of his material points rather, as Ganivet himself admits, to an island-like spirit of aggression. Moreover, since the country's geological formation is for Ganivet the main influence on national character, it has been necessary to point out that until relatively modern times—indeed, up to the very threshold of Spain's admitted 'aggression'— the history of the Iberian peninsula reveals a 'resistance'- prompting juxtaposition of separate states rather than the millennia of 'peninsular' conditions required by Ganivet's theory.

So far I have objected to Ganivet's notion of the territorial spirit on his own chosen ground; that of the trio
England, France and Spain. However, since Ganivet bases
his views on general geological conditions, it is relevant
to test those views by reference to other countries that are
not mentioned by him or which are mentioned only incidentally. And here one can fall back on one's own
general notions of world history. Which are the peoples
that suggest themselves most readily as aggressive powers?
The following are a few that immediately come to mind:
the Persians under Cyrus, Darius and Xerxes, the Mace-
donians under Alexander, the Romans, the Germanic
tribes, the Huns under Attila, the Turks, the Arabs, the
Spaniards, the French, the English, the Germans. Only
one of these is an island people: the English, whom
Ganivet takes as his example of the aggressive island
spirit. The Romans (and the Carthaginians) he mentions
as aggressive peoples, but he forestalls criticism on their
account by the following claim:

> Cuando el espíritu territorial no está aún formado le suple el
> espíritu político; esto es, el de ciudadanía; y cuando esta
> llega a tomar cuerpo, se semeja al insular, porque el hombre
> que vive en un recinto cerrado o amurallado considera que
> forma como un cuerpo distinto del territorio. Roma y
> Cartago fueron ciudades insulares; su poder agresivo fue
> tan grande como escasa su fuerza para resistir (178).

Did the city spirit of aggression, then, precede the territorial spirit, the city precede the geological formation?
And if it evolved from it, how did peninsular or continental peoples come to establish a way of life so out of
harmony with their territorial spirit and nevertheless prosper? And is it not surprising, still judging the matter from

Ganivet's own determinist standpoint, that a spirit of citizenship should in a few hundred years transform a territorial spirit of geological dimensions?

Ganivet mentions the Arabs, too, as aggressors in their occupation of Spain, but here he accepts the fact without advancing any explanation. Captivated by his method, one is tempted to give oneself up to the sheer joy—and folly— of this type of intellectual fantasy and suggest a reason. Did the Arabs not come from the vast desert areas where men live as though on islands in their isolated oases? And one can carry the speculation over to other countries. If France must be admitted as an aggressive power, must it not be because France developed in successive stages outwards from Paris, and is not that character-imprinting nucleus still known today as the *Île de France*, the *island* of France? And in Germany, did the aggressiveness perhaps come, originally, from that isolated island of East Prussia, separated by Poland and Danzig from the rest of the country? Alas, in these cases of aggression, as in all the other cases listed above but not enlarged upon, the truth is probably far less intellectually satisfying and far more emotionally depressing, for the truth is, perhaps, that every nation has been aggressive when the advantages have appeared likely to outweigh the losses, and that, it seems, has little or nothing to do with any form of territorial spirit.

CRUSADING FERVOUR AND THE SPIRIT OF INDEPENDENCE

So far in this chapter I have examined the two 'fuerzas constituyentes' that Ganivet claims to be fundamental in Spanish national character: stoicism and the territorial spirit of independence. Now I shall show how Ganivet

brings them together to explain Spain's past and to offer
guidance for the future. But I must first recall and emphasize my findings on his case for stoicism, for if Ganivet
shows anything with his arguments on pages 152–7, it is
not that stoicism is a peculiarly Spanish characteristic run-
ning through the whole of Spanish civilization, but rather
that it is a general characteristic of western and southern
Europe at a particular moment in time. Moreover, it is
not stoicism that subsequently appears as the all-important
partner to the spirit of independence; it is the crusading
fervour of Christianity, which according to Ganivet developed from stoicism under Arabic influence (157–73,
especially 160–2). Thus, from page 187 onwards the two
main 'fuerzas constituyentes' of the Spanish soul with
which Ganivet operates are not stoicism and the spirit of
independence, but crusading fervour and the spirit of
independence.[1]

As an illustration of this we can consider pages 187–
222, in which, having affirmed his two fundamental
'fuerzas constituyentes', Ganivet shows Spanish character
in action in three different spheres. The first concerns
military organization (or warrior lack of organization) and
it shows Ganivet's thought at its most lucid: he starts
from what he believes to be the inescapable national
spirit of independence and he advocates a solution in
harmony with that spirit.[2] Neither stoicism nor crusading
fervour is mentioned, for here the spirit of independence
alone suffices for Ganivet's argument. Stoicism, however,

[1] For the sole mention of stoicism after p. 187 see what follows above.
[2] Ganivet's thought, here, is lucid, I have said. Nevertheless, his conclusion is a platitude. Probably every platoon commander in every army
in the world—island, peninsular and continental—has had pressed upon
him the need for his platoon to be able to operate as a self-contained and
'independent' unit, whether it be for 'resistance' or for 'aggression'.

is mentioned in his second example: Spain, he says, is characterized by an idealistic approach to legal matters and this is because of the common influence of Christian feeling and Senecan philosophy 'en cuanto ambos son concordantes' (204): morality is rigid but offenders are treated with lenience. Stoicism would appear to join hands with crusading fervour when Ganivet thereupon cites Don Quixote as a representative of this transcendental 'justicia española', in contrast to Sancho Panza, the apparently un-Spanish upholder of the 'justicia vulgar de los códigos y tribunales' (205).[1] In Ganivet's third example of Spanish character in action, in his pages on Spanish art, stoicism is left aside and it is now mysticism (fervour) that is placed beside the spirit of independence as the most powerful determining factor. Stoicism is not mentioned again in the whole book; throughout Sections B and C its place is taken by the crusading fervour that Spain is alleged to have acquired through centuries of Arabic occupation and Arabic contacts. It is this crusading fervour that is henceforth upheld by Ganivet as the true partner to the territorial spirit of independence.

But this brings us to what is perhaps the gravest criticism of the *Idearium*, and the case is surely indisputable. The crusading fervour and the spirit of independence that, between them, underlie all Ganivet's diagnosis and

[1] There is a clear conflict between the interpretation that Ganivet here gives of Sancho, and his statement, a few pages earlier, that 'mientras un español permanezca ligado a las clases proletarias, que son el archivo y el depósito de los sentimientos inexplicables, profundos, de un país, no puede ser hombre de ley con la gravedad y aplomo que la naturaleza del asunto requiere' (203). Moreover, his suggestion that Sancho is, in contrast to his master, un-Spanish in his attitude to justice would appear to be contradicted by his reference, later in the book, to 'el prudente Sancho Panza, que era tan español y tan manchego como Don Quijote' (238). It is, of course, yet another example of how Ganivet bends facts to the needs of his argument.

prescription in Sections B and C represent, in fact, mutually opposing incentives to action. On the one hand there
is the crusading fervour that calls for expansion; on the
other hand there is the territorial spirit of independence
that demands withdrawal. Once one admits the existence
of these two conflicting forces—and Ganivet has not made
a convincing case for either of them—one can explain,
from Ganivet's determinist standpoint, any general tendency in the external policy of any country. If a country
conquered, one can say it was acting in accordance with
its crusading fervour; if it failed, one can maintain it was
acting against its native spirit of independence. Since
Ganivet was concerned with a country that had apparently
failed in the business of power politics, he necessarily
emphasized the infringement of the country's spirit of independence. But let us imagine that Spain had succeeded
in Latin America and had become the centre of a pros-
perous empire. Would not Ganivet then have been able
to attribute it to the country's crusading zeal? See his
review of Spain's foreign adventures: to the North, East
and West her external policy has failed through disregard
of the peninsular spirit of independence; only the Southern
policy was not attempted; here, says Ganivet, was the
proper direction of our external action:

> Yo entiendo que la política africana era muy natural después
> de terminada la Reconquista, y si a ella hubiéramos con-
> sagrado todas las fuerzas nacionales, hubiéramos fundado un
> poder político indestructible, tanto porque nacía lógica-
> mente de nuestra historia medieval, cuanto porque no
> hubiera chocado con los intereses de Europa (275).

We cannot affirm he is wrong. Perhaps Spain's medieval
crusading spirit would have established an indestructible

Spanish empire in Africa. But if it had been attempted, and if it had failed, Ganivet would still, with his dual basis of study, have been able to explain that failure and attribute it to a violation of the country's inescapable spirit of independence—and to the African people's continental spirit of resistance. And if the other three directions of action had not been attempted, Ganivet could still have affirmed, as he does here with Africa, that Spain's medieval history—and especially her championing of Christianity—demanded action northwards, westwards and eastwards, and he could likewise have revelled in the joyful hypothesis of Spanish successes in all those fields. In this respect, his comment on Napoleon's campaigns is relevant:

> Y es mi sentir que Napoleón pudo, concentrando todas sus fuerzas, asaltar, destruir Inglaterra y acaso domar España, pero que no hubiera podido jamás triunfar de la resistencia pasiva de Rusia (180).

If we substitute *los Reyes Católicos y sus sucesores* for *Napoleón*, *Italia* for *España*, and *Africa* for *Rusia*, we have ready-made the sort of comment we might expect from Ganivet if Spain's external policy had taken a completely different course: if a vigorously pursued southern policy had ended in failure and if the absence of serious involvement elsewhere allowed patriotic hypotheses of glorious success in those other directions.[1]

---

[1] There is a similarly flexible duality in Ganivet's treatment of Philip II:

> [In the policy of Philip II] había un error capital: el de haber dirigido la acción de nuestro país por caminos ajenos a nuestros intereses [the spirit of independence]; pero había, asimismo, un pensamiento admirable: el de inspirar esa acción en los sentimientos genuinamente españoles ['su empeño en sostener las ideas católicas'; crusading fervour] (259).

Again one sees clearly the easy shift of emphasis that could have been made if Philip II's policy had been successful, and one recalls forcibly—

For Ganivet is an armchair Don Quixote, and burns with the crusading fervour that he believes to be fundamental in Spanish character:

> ¿Puede darse nada más bello que civilizar salvajes, que conquistar nuevos pueblos a nuestra religión, a nuestras leyes y a nuestro idioma? (260).

Again and again we glimpse his fantasies of imperialism and conquest. But Spain has tried to project such fantasies on to the material world and has failed. Ganivet is satisfied to test the knightly helmet no more; he is content to ponder the glories that might have been and to urge those glories that call for intellectual rather than material action. He is forced by his realization of Spain's economic position to urge that the path of material conquest be renounced. He even suggests—though in muted terms and perhaps without complete conviction—that Spain's imperial exploits were mistaken. But he clings tenaciously to the ground that Spain still holds, especially in the Hispanic world. He champions Spanish colonization in Latin America against English colonization in North America, and if he calls for the concentration of Spanish energies within the Peninsula, it is as a means of enabling the country to

---

here as elsewhere above—Karl Popper's criticism of J. S. Mill: 'A method that can explain everything that might happen explains nothing' (*The Poverty of Historicism*, London 1957, p. 154). E. H. Carr's observation, too, is worth noting: the 'game of historical "might-have-beens",' he declares, is 'the favourite consolation of the defeated' (*What is History?*, Cambridge Trevelyan Lectures, London 1961, p. 93). In this respect Ganivet's own confession is perhaps relevant: 'De aquí que no pudiendo intervenir [in Africa], como no podemos materialmente, se me haya ocurrido a mí intervenir con la pluma' (II, 913). He is referring to the writing of *La conquista del reino de Maya*, but the words seem relevant also to the *Idearium*.

forge ideas of her own with which to lead Hispanic peoples
everywhere:

> Importante es la acción de una raza por medio de la fuerza,
> pero es más importante su acción ideal; y esta alcanza solo
> su apogeo cuando se abandona la acción exterior y se con-
> centra dentro del territorio toda la vitalidad nacional (225).

> Necesitamos reconstituir nuestras fuerzas materiales para
> resolver nuestros asuntos interiores, y nuestra fuerza ideal
> para influir en la esfera de nuestros legítimos intereses ex-
> ternos, para fortificar nuestro prestigio en los pueblos de
> origen hispánico (266–7).

Here, then, after serving as opposite poles with which to
explain and judge Spanish history, the spirit of independence and the crusading fervour come together. Through
the concentration of energies that only independence can
give, Spain will find again an outlet for her crusading zeal.
Here, says Ganivet, lies the nation's true greatness and its
true destiny, its 'fuerza ideal' and its 'acción ideal'.

If only Ganivet did not have to ignore so many historical facts and ride roughshod over so much logic in order
to arrive at this conclusion. Nor does he only *ignore* historical facts. There is evidence, too, that he distorts or
misinterprets the relatively few facts that he does cite in
his work, for almost every one of them has prompted
objections from one quarter or another. Thus, it has been
alleged that Ganivet lays too much emphasis on stoicism[1]
and confuses Senecan pagan morality with Christianity.[2]
And there have been claims that he exaggerates Arabic

---

[1] QS, pp. 170–3; Manuel Durán, 'Ganivet y el senequismo hispánico',
in *Insula* Nos. 228–9 (November–December 1965), 'Todo lo demás (es
decir, la tesis del estoicismo hispano),' writes Durán, 'es equívoco,
confusión, abuso del lenguaje, extensión indebida de ideas, situaciones o
parecidos superficiales.'   [2] Unamuno, *OC* IV, 1958, 965.

influence,[1] misinterprets the Reconquest,[2] and overlooks
the fact that mysticism and fanaticism, far from being
specifically Spanish characteristics, occurred earlier and
more notably in other parts of Europe.[3] And allegations
that he misinterprets the Reformation[4] and presents a
completely false view of the development of the Catholic
Church.[5] And evidence that he distorts the Spanish
Golden Age[6] and perhaps misconstrues Philip II's role in
the country's decline.[7] And a suggestion that he overlooks
the importance of social and economic influences.[8] And
objections to his interpretation of the *fueros*[9] and of the
revolt of the *comuneros*.[10] Evidence of this kind cannot be

[1] Unamuno, *OC* IV, 1958, 966, 988–9; MFA, p. 115; Pedro Sáinz y
Rodríguez, *La evolución de las ideas sobre la decadencia española*, Madrid
[1925], p. 83; Hans Jeschke, in *Revue Hispanique* LXII, 1928, 188.

[2] Rafael Altamira, *Psicología del pueblo español*, 2nd ed., Barcelona [1918],
p. 110.

[3] Altamira, op. cit., pp. 105–6; Jeschke, op. cit., pp. 188–9. See also
Sáinz y Rodríguez, op. cit., p. 83.

[4] Unamuno, *OC* IV, 1958, 966 (Ganivet judges the Reformation 'con
notoria injusticia y a mi entender con algún desconocimiento de su
íntima esencia').

[5] C. Mª. Abad, in *Razón y Fe* LXXII (May-August 1925), especially pp.
198–200 ('Sencillamente Ganivet en estas primeras páginas del *Idearium*
se pone a hablar de lo que no ha estudiado y no es extraño que diga
tonterías'); Rafael García y García de Castro, *Los 'intelectuales' y la Iglesia*,
Madrid 1934, pp. 202–3.

[6] Manuel Azaña, *Plumas y palabras*, Madrid 1930, pp. 19–49 (supported
by Angel del Río and M. J. Bernardete in *El concepto contemporáneo de
España*, Buenos Aires 1946, p. 379); Antonio Espina, *Ganivet, el hombre y
la obra*, 3rd ed., Buenos Aires, 1954, pp. 56–8.

[7] Altamira, op. cit., p. 109; Espina, op. cit., p. 37.

[8] Unamuno, *OC* IV, 1958, 963, 992–3.

[9] Altamira, op. cit., p. 110 ('palpables errores históricos'); Sáinz y
Rodríguez, op. cit., p. 83.

[10] Azaña, op. cit., pp. 49–87 ('otro ejemplo del poder analítico de
Ganivet,' he comments ironically, p. 49). See also the view of more
recent historians on the *comuneros*, reviewed in Joseph Pérez's 'Pour
une nouvelle interprétation des *Comunidades* de Castille' (in *BH* 65,
1963, 238–83). 'Azaña,' he says, 'a fait justice des brillantes improvisa-
tions de Ganivet' (p. 265). According to José Antonio Maravall the aims
of the *comuneros* were primarily constitutional and social (*Las Comunidades
de Castilla: una primera revolución moderna*, Madrid 1963).

dismissed lightly, especially since it all relates to one or other of the two 'fuerzas constituyentes' that Ganivet claims to be central to Spanish civilization and upon which he then bases his recommendations for the country's future.[1] For the *Idearium*, however unsatisfactory it may be in facts and logic, is not as unsystematic a work as is usually alleged; on the contrary, as I shall show more fully in my next chapter, it is a work of naïve determinism in which everything is claimed to form part of a vast network of causal relationships. Nothing, Ganivet believes, is irrelevant to the rest; 'todo existe por algo y para algo' (264). To do as some critics have done (including several of those just referred to)—to undermine one or both the pillars in this system, the allegedly central and all-sustaining 'fuerzas constituyentes' of the Spanish soul, and then to accept the author's conclusions—is to misunderstand the character of the work. It is also, perhaps, a sign that critical faculties have been intoxicated by the 'patriotic' conclusions offered. But I shall examine this suggestion more fully in my final chapter when I consider reasons for the work's remarkable success.

My findings so far are these: that Ganivet's case for the two 'fuerzas constituyentes' discussed in this chapter, and in particular his upholding of them as the central forces of Spanish civilization, is supported by no clear evidence and by much inadequate reasoning and must therefore be

---

[1] One can note here another observation by Karl Popper:
the discovery of instances which confirm a theory means very little if we have not tried, and failed, to discover refutations. For if we are uncritical we shall always find what we want: we shall look for, and find, confirmations, and we shall look away from, and not see, whatever might be dangerous to our pet theories. In this way it is only too easy to obtain what appears to be overwhelming evidence in favour of a theory which, if approached critically, would have been refuted (*The Poverty of Historicism*, p. 134).

G

considered not proven; further, that since Ganivet's recommendations for the future of Spain are based upon
these alleged central forces, it follows that they also lack
the factual and logical support that the author pretends to
give them. If Spain's proper policy should be to concentrate her energies within national frontiers and make herself the spiritual leader of the Hispanic world, this must
certainly be shown by arguments different from those put
forward in *Idearium español*.

But reference to Spain's 'proper policy' is misleading,
for the duality of independence and crusading fervour
proposed by Ganivet allows the reader considerable freedom to take his stand where he will, to invoke now one
force and now the other in his review of Spanish history,
and to invoke now one force and now the other in a consideration of Spain's present and future. The historian is
offered a theory that will adapt itself easily to facts, and
the politician a theory that will adapt itself easily to passions. 'La guerra de Africa,' wrote Ganivet, 'es una prueba
patente de que la política africana no está apoyada aún por
intereses vitales de nuestra nación' (276). These words
have been quoted frequently in support of a policy of non-
intervention in Africa, with emphasis on Spain's alleged
territorial spirit of independence; they have also been
quoted, with italicization of the word *aún*, in support of a
policy of intervention, as is demanded by the nation's
alleged crusading fervour. I find the inference unavoidable: the ambiguity of the *Idearium* and its consequent
limited value as a guide to Spanish destinies has, rather
ironically, been one of the principal reasons for its wide
success. This point, too, I shall examine more fully in my
final chapter.

IV

IDEARIUM ESPAÑOL
AS A DETERMINIST SYSTEM

Ganivet's thought, as it is revealed to us in the *Idearium*, is basically determinist. A given civilization, he suggests, is a geographically localized configuration of interrelated and interdependent social, political, religious and artistic phenomena, in which 'everything that happens has a cause or causes, and could not have happened differently unless something in the cause or causes had also been different'.[1] Apart from the manifest neglect, here, of temporal localization—for Spanish civilization in the twentieth century, one might expect, will probably be nearer to English civilization of the same period than to the civilization of medieval Spain—I find this to be a useful working hypothesis. It does not, however, carry us very far towards a solution of the problems with which the student of civilization is in fact concerned. Beyond the hypothesis of determinism one must consider also the application of this hypothesis in particular cases. It is with one such application, albeit an extremely naïve one, that we are concerned in the following pages.

My first point follows from my findings in the previous two chapters: despite his view of Spanish civilization as a configuration of interrelated and interdependent phenomena, Ganivet shows no awareness of the enormous complexity of that configuration (unless it be to reject it as

[1] In the latter half of my sentence I incorporate the definition of determinism proposed by E. H. Carr (in *What is History?*, p. 87).

93

impure), nor of the manner in which those different phenomena interact upon one another in generation after
generation, nor of the occasional profound—and re-
orientating—effect of influences from outside Spain since
the Moslem occupation. Intellectual advances are notably
absent from his review, and as for history as progress
through the transmission of acquired skills from one
generation to another, he will have none of it: 'su valor
ideal es nulo,' he declares (165); 'cuando acierto a levantarme siquiera dos palmos sobre las vulgaridades rutinarias
que me rodean y siento el calor y la luz de alguna idea
grande y pura, todas esas bellas invenciones no me sirven
para nada' (166). Instead, Ganivet sets up triumphantly
his notion of dual—and ultimately opposing—'fuerzas
constituyentes' that run through the whole of Spanish
history like Darwin's 'hidden bonds of connection'
through animal species,[1] and give the people, and thence
also their civilization, their essential and inescapable
character.

And here, in my reference to Darwin's *Origin of Species*,
I have touched upon what I take to be a particular characteristic of Ganivet's approach to civilization and one that
narrows considerably the broad meaning of determinism
that I accepted in my opening paragraph. For Ganivet's
determinism is clearly that of the age in which he lived,
strongly influenced by the notion of natural evolution and
natural selection, and with consequent emphasis both on
physical environment as the all-important, ever-present,
inescapable formative influence and, thence also, on the
need to adapt oneself to the demands of that physical
environment if one is to survive and prosper. And here,
of course, we recognize immediately Ganivet's two main

[1] Charles Darwin, *On the Origin of Species* . . ., London 1859, p. 433.

aims in the *Idearium*: to indicate the national character that has been imposed on Spain, across the centuries, by her own physical environment, and to urge upon his readers recognition of this character and obedience to it so that the nation may realize its true potential.

But before we consider in greater detail the implications of this approach, we must ask ourselves how Ganivet himself arrived at it. I have found no evidence that he had any direct contact with the writings of natural scientists, though he does refer to *darwinismo* in his first doctorate thesis (II, 639), without apparently being influenced by it in that thesis or the next. He would presumably be aware of contemporary debates on the subject of evolutionism, at least during his stay in Antwerp, but here too the evidence is slight. What is clear, however, is that during his stay in Antwerp Ganivet was reading 'de cabo a rabo y con bastante más satisfacción que las de Renan' (II, 829), the works of the French determinist historian and philosopher, Hippolyte Taine (1828–93), one of the principal writers of the time to apply the concepts of natural science to the study of civilization, and was even attempting, in his letters, to apply Taine's methods to aspects of Belgian life that he observed around him. In the *Idearium*, I believe, the similarities with Taine, and even the influence of Taine, are clear. I shall show this briefly in the following pages whilst illustrating Ganivet's determinism. Since Taine is an acknowledged determinist and Ganivet is not, such similarities as I find will serve also, apart from their intrinsic interest, to strengthen my case for Ganivet's own determinism.[1]

[1] Taine's influence on Ganivet has recently been disputed by Segundo Serrano Poncela (*'El secreto de Melibea' y otros ensayos*, Madrid 1959, pp. 88–91). Elsewhere I consider the evidence more fully than is possible in

But one must start by indicating a difference. Ganivet, like Taine, insists that a given civilization is a configuration of interrelated phenomena. Also like Taine, he emphasizes the need to discover the all-pervading characteristic of that configuration (its 'disposition primitive', its 'fuerza dominante y céntrica'), and to show how this all-pervading characteristic reveals itself in different aspects of the civilization in question. He does not, however, accept Taine's celebrated trio of *race*, *milieu* and *moment* to explain that central characteristic and its repercussions at a given moment in time. Not that he omits to mention *race* and *milieu*; on the contrary, they are essential to his study. But *milieu* for Ganivet is merely geographical—or, rather, geological—*milieu*, unchanging across the ages, and *race* he sees simply as the product of

---

this chapter and establish the following three stages in the development of Ganivet's determinism:

1. In his two doctorate theses (1888–9) Ganivet viewed a given civilization as a system of interrelated parts, with a fundamental all-pervading national *modo de ser*, but did not attempt to explain why one national *modo de ser* should be different from another, nor to define any particular *modo de ser*.

2. In his *Epistolario* (1893–5), apparently as a result of his reading of Taine, Ganivet went a step further in his determinism and emphasized the importance of physical environment on personal, regional and national *modos de ser*, but still did not define clearly any particular *modo de ser*.

3. In *Idearium español* (1896) he took yet another step and arrived at a clear notion of the *espíritu territorial*, 'una fuerza dominante y céntrica donde pudiera decirse que está alojado el ideal de cada raza':

Là s'arrête la recherche; on est tombé sur quelque disposition primitive, sur quelque trait propre à toutes les sensations, à toutes les conceptions d'un siècle ou d'une race, sur quelque particularité inséparable de toutes les démarches de son esprit et de son cœur (Taine, *Histoire de la littérature anglaise*, I, Paris 1877, xvii).

'Angel Ganivet and Hippolyte Taine' (to be published shortly).

In the present chapter I shall confine my Taine references to the author's most celebrated 'manifesto': the 1863 Introduction to his *Histoire de la littérature anglaise* [hereafter *HLA*, I, with quotation from the fourth edition, Paris 1877].

that *milieu*. In short, *race* and *milieu* are fused by Ganivet into a single immutable force. Significantly, the term 'faculté maîtresse', by which Taine refers to a given civilization's 'disposition primitive,' has its counterpart in Ganivet's purely geological term, 'espíritu territorial'.

Perhaps this difference of approach has its origin in the difference of emphasis of the two writers, for Taine is concerned primarily to explain what happened in the past and Ganivet is concerned far more with predicting what should happen in the future. A theory that admits the influence of ever-changing social, intellectual and technological *milieux* is manifestly less useful as an instrument of prediction than one that admits only the immutable and ever-insistent demands of geology. Be this as it may, Ganivet's determinism is clearly a far cruder example than Taine's of 'that pseudogeographical determinism which is today once for all discredited'.[1]

But we have seen the difficulty that faces Ganivet if he accepts the territorial spirit of independence as his only guide: he is unable to justify Spain's claim to *ideal* leadership in Latin America (above, pp. 65–7). And we have examined his response to this problem: his hypothesis of stoicism evolving to fervour under the influence of the Moslem occupation (above, pp. 70–4). Moreover, in this hypothesis he admits the influence both of non-geographical *milieu* and of *moment*.[2] What he does not mention at this

---

[1] Marc Bloch, *The Historian's Craft*, Manchester University Press, 1963, p. 196.

[2] Elsewhere, too, he admits the significance of *moment*, notably in the transformation of the Spanish territorial spirit from independence to aggression. But because of his emphasis on the immutable influence of *race-milieu* he can accept this transformation only as a temporary—and regrettable—deviation of Spanish history from the 'cauce que le estaba marcado' (219). The demands of 'the marked-out path' are inexorable and must eventually prevail.

point, however, is *race* and geographical *milieu*. The treatment is still determinist, but it is Hegelian rather than Darwinian determinism and the passage as a whole stands out from the biological pretence of the rest of the book like a magical and providential *deus ex machina*—which, of course, is exactly what it is.

I have just referred to 'biological pretence', and I must seek to justify myself. Ganivet's view of civilization, I have claimed, was strongly influenced—even if only indirectly, through Taine—by contemporary debates on natural evolution. Let us consider evidence from the *Idearium*:

> La síntesis espiritual de un país es su arte. Pudiera decirse que el espíritu territorial es la medula; la religión, el cerebro; el espíritu guerrero, el corazón; el espíritu jurídico, la musculatura, y el espíritu artístico, como una red nerviosa que todo lo enlaza y lo unifica y lo mueve (209).

We need not take his parallels too seriously (indeed, like several other images in the *Idearium*, they misrepresent his thought). It is sufficient to see in them an indication of the author's view of civilization as an organism of interdependent parts. Moreover, like plant and animal species for the natural historian, so also social organisms for Ganivet are moulded by their physical environment. The guiding principle of all peoples, he affirms, is self-preservation ('la conservación'), but this principle manifests itself differently in different environments (176–7). The territorial spirit is the natural response of a given people to a particular geological setting. And because it is the natural response, it is also the most adequate response and must therefore be accepted as the necessary basis of the civilization of that particular group. The territorial spirit can never be totally suppressed, Ganivet believes, and attempts at suppression lead inevitably to weakness, indecision and deformed growth. Everything must stem naturally from the fundamental territorial spirit: 'un poder que no brota espontáneo de la fuerza natural y efectiva de una nación es un palo en manos de un ciego' (257–8). Discover that 'fuerza natural', then, and act in accordance with its dictates; accept reality, 'la realidad de los hechos' (which Ganivet equates with 'la ley natural', 208); consider the position of Spain in its process of 'natural evolución' (281); conform to 'las leyes naturales' (281); ensure that the future organization of Spain is adapted to the nation's 'constitución natural' (197). Again and again Ganivet presses his point. It is the only way in which one can profitably influence the course of historical events: 'conociendo la realidad y sometiéndose a ella, no pretendiendo trastrocarla ni burlarla' (243). The insistent centre of that reality, the necessary centre of any adequate national synthesis, is the territorial spirit.

Ganivet, then, like Taine, approaches the study of civilization with concepts and terminology derived from the natural sciences.[1] But whereas the natural scientist is concerned with the physical aspects of organic life, Taine and Ganivet, in their probing of social organisms, emphasize the alleged underlying psychology: 'l'histoire au fond est un *problème de psychologie*' (*HLA*, I, xlv). 'Los pueblos tienen personalidad, estilo o manera como los artistas' (212), says Ganivet; 'las sociedades tienen personalidad, ideas, energías' (292). And it is Ganivet's initial aim in *Idearium español* to define the basic elements in Spanish

[1] Aujourd'hui, l'histoire comme la zoologie a trouvé son anatomie, et quelle que soit la branche historique à laquelle on s'attache, philologie, linguistique ou mythologie, c'est par cette voie qu'on travaille à lui faire produire de nouveaux fruits (*HLA*, I, xii).

character: first, stoicism; then, the territorial spirit of independence. Seneca and Spain's 'constitución ideal', the
psychological study of an individual and the psychological
study of a country—Ganivet passes easily between one
and the other:

> El problema más difícil de resolver en el estudio psicológico
> [. . .] es el de enlazar, con rigor lógico, la experiencia interna
> con los fenómenos exteriores [. . .].
> *De igual modo,* cuando se estudia la estructura psicológica
> de un país, no basta representar el mecanismo externo [. . .];
> hay que ir más hondo y buscar en la realidad misma el
> núcleo irreducible al que están adheridas todas las envueltas
> que van transformando en el tiempo la fisonomía de este
> país (173-5; my italics).

Similarly, later in his work, Ganivet seeks to justify his
'aplicación de la psicología individual a los estados sociales,
y la patología del espíritu a la patología política' (288) and
he offers himself as Spain's 'médico espiritual' (286). For
Spain, he believes, is mentally ill.[1] The fundamental
national spirit has been suppressed and the nation has
therefore lost its true path. Phenomena are no longer seen
in their proper perspective. Ganivet invokes clinical
authority for his use of the term aboulia to describe such a
state, establishes 'una relación de causalidad' between the
different symptoms, and accepting, as he himself says, the
positivist term 'sentido sintético', he attributes the alleged
aboulia of Spain to 'la debilitación del sentido sintético,
de la facultad de asociar las representaciones' (286-91).
His prescription for cure follows logically from his diag-

---

[1] On Taine's similar views—of France as a sick patient, of himself as
'médecin consultant' and of his history of France as 'une consultation de
médecins'—see Benedetto Croce, *History as the Story of Liberty,* London
1941, pp. 187-95.

nosis: stimulate the national faculty for synthesis by recognizing and accepting the necessary centre of such a synthesis, the 'núcleo irreducible al que están adheridas todas las envueltas' (175), the 'fuerza dominante y céntrica donde pudiera decirse que está alojado el ideal de cada raza' (211). We are back once more to the territorial spirit as the necessary and only adequate response to the struggle for existence.

So far I have emphasized Ganivet's view of national character as a product of environment. But as national character is a product, so also it is a producer, and the territorial spirit of independence reveals itself clearly and insistently, for Ganivet, in the different manifestations of Spanish character through the ages: primarily in the ideas and feelings and beliefs of the common people and in their reactions to different circumstances; but also in more specialized fields: in philosophy, in science, in law, in the arts, in literature, and in the transformations that imported elements of civilization—'la religión cristiana, el arte griego y la ley romana' (211)—have undergone in their Spanish environment. Complemented at need by that other all-important national characteristic, stoicism or Christian fervour, the spirit of independence presses itself constantly in *Idearium español* as the necessary guide to all adequate national action. I recall, for illustration, the three fields that Ganivet discusses in the second half of Section A as evidence of Spanish character in action: military organization, justice and the arts.

1. *Military organization*: 'España es por esencia, *porque así lo exige el espíritu de su territorio,* un pueblo guerrero, no un pueblo militar' (187; my italics). Ganivet finds evidence for his belief in the fact that the national figure of the Reconquest was not a true king or a sage or a saint, but

the Cid, 'un rey ambulante, un guerrillero que trabaja por cuenta propia' (188), in the fact that the great military figure during Spain's Italian campaigns was 'un capitán nada más, el Gran Capitán' (188), in the form taken by the Spanish conquest of America ('los conquistadores, en cuanto hombres de armas, fueron legítimos guerrilleros, lo mismo los más bajos que los más altos, sin exceptuar a Hernán Cortés', 189), in the alleged reaction of the Spanish people in times of crisis ('la insubordinación de todas las clases sociales', 194). In all fields, he suggests, Spanish civilization has flourished in so far as the spirit of independence has been the guiding force, and this is true of the spiritual world as it is of the material world: Cervantes and Loyola were 'tan conquistadores como Cortés o Pizarro' (190). Consequently, the spirit of independence must be the principal guide in the future also, and in the field of military organization as elsewhere the spirit of independence must be the necessary basis. Hence Ganivet's recommendation that the Spanish army should be composed basically of small combat units. 'Véase,' he urges, 'cómo una idea que parece vaga e inaprisionable como la del espíritu del territorio, lleva en sí la solución de grandes problemas políticos' (196).

2. *Justice*: Spain, like other European countries, has inherited Roman and Germanic laws. But it is not the written system of laws that is important, but the way in which those laws are interpreted by men, according their own inner 'ley ideal superior, la ley constante de interpretación jurídica, que en España ha sido más bien de disolución jurídica' (200). The Spanish reaction to justice, Ganivet continues, 'es algo muy hondo que *no está en nuestra mano arrancar*' (202; my italics). 'Mientras un español permanezca ligado a las clases proletarias, que son el archivo y el

depósito de los sentimientos inexplicables, profundos, de un país, no puede ser hombre de ley con la gravedad y aplomo que la naturaleza del asunto requiere' (203). Again Ganivet cites Cervantes in support of his case (205). Moreover, judges themselves are inevitably affected by the general national attitude to justice:

> No se piense que estas ideas se quedan en el aire, en el ambiente social, sin ejercer influjo en la administración de justicia: por muy rectos que sean los jueces y por muy claros que sean los códigos, no hay medio de que un juez se abstraiga por completo de la sociedad en que vive, ni es posible impedir que por entre los preceptos de la ley se infiltre el espíritu del pueblo a quien se aplica; y ese espíritu, con labor sorda, invisible y, por tanto, inevitable, concluye por destruir el sentido que las leyes tenían en su origen, procediendo con tanta cautela que, sin tocar a una coma de los textos legales, les obliga a decir, si conviene, lo contrario de lo que antes habían dicho (206).

'Tenemos, pues, un régimen anómalo, en armonía con nuestro carácter' (206). Castile's support for Isabella against Juana la Beltraneja at the end of the Reconquest revealed a characteristic disregard of written laws, and led to the establishment of the Spanish nation.

3. *The Arts*: Art is the 'spiritual synthesis' of a country and each people must find the form of expression most suited to its native genius:

> Nuestras ideas, si se atiende a su origen, son las mismas que las de los demás pueblos de Europa, los cuales, con mejor o peor derecho, han sido partícipes del caudal hereditario legado por la antigüedad; pero la combinación que nosotros hemos hecho de esas ideas es nuestra, propia y exclusiva, y es diferente de la que han hecho los demás, por ser diferentes nuestro clima y nuestra raza (211).

The Spanish spirit is religious and artistic, and the best
scientists of Spain are those who feel themselves 'arras-
trados hacia las alturas donde la ciencia se desnaturaliza,
combinándose ya con la religión, ya con el arte' (212).
Now the content of Spanish art, says Ganivet, comes from
the nation's 'constitución ideal', and the technique from
the territorial spirit (212). Whether it be Velázquez or
Goya or any other Spanish artist great or small, one notes
the same lack of technical reflexion and the artist's sur-
render to his own personal impulse: 'es constante y es
universal en nuestro arte, porque brota espontáneo de
nuestro amor a la independencia' (213–14). Again, Ganivet
thinks of Cervantes, 'el más grande de todos los conquistadores', and of his typically Spanish masterpiece
'nuestra obra típica, la obra por antonomasia' (214). And
he thinks of the genius of Lope de Vega and the subsequent 'abismos insondables' of the Spanish theatre in the
eighteenth century. The blame for such decadence, he
affirms, is Lope's, 'y más que de Lope, de nuestro carácter'
(216). 'Nuestro carácter, en cuanto a la técnica artística, es
un exaltado amor a la independencia, que nos lleva a no
hacer caso de nadie' (216). But it is something that cannot
be avoided:

> Lo más interesante en estas anomalías que de nuestro carác-
> ter provienen, es que *no hay medio de evitarlas*, imitando los
> buenos modelos y formando escuelas artísticas [. . .]. *Ten-*
> *dremos, como siempre*, obras magistrales creadas por los
> maestros y una rápida degradación provocada por la audacia
> y desenfado de los aprendices [. . .]. En vez de formar un
> ejército literario, no somos más que una partida de gue-
> rrilleros de las letras (217–18; my italics).

Ganivet recommends a solution in harmony with the
Spanish spirit—and with his determinist beliefs: let artists

develop their regional roots. As the Spanish national spirit abandoned its proper path, 'el cauce que le estaba marcado' (219), so also artists have abandoned their native environments. Their energies must be united upon the basis of the reality in which they live.

Military organization, justice, and the arts. But these are only three of the many fields where Ganivet's determinism reveals itself in *Idearium español*. He will admit nothing as irrelevant to his system, nothing as fortuitous or purely spontaneous. 'Todo existe por algo y para algo' (264). The many different aspects of Spanish civilization that Ganivet presents to us are held to be motivated by and ultimately to stem from Spanish national character, and this national character, in its turn, is seen as the product of natural conditions, being a local response to the general principle of self-preservation.[1] But Spain's foreign policy, Ganivet finds, is out of harmony with the spirit of independence that reveals itself in other fields; it has abandoned its proper path, and the country has assumed an aggressive role. The outcome was inevitable:

Al empeñarse España, nación peninsular, en proceder como las naciones continentales, se condenaba a una ruina cierta, puesto que, si una nación se fortifica adquiriendo nuevos territorios que están dentro de su esfera de acción natural, se debilita en cambio con la agregación de otros que llevan consigo contingencias desfavorables a sus intereses propios y permanentes (226).

[1] Similarly, if England is aggressive, 'no es obra de la voluntad; arranca de la constitución del territorio' (178); and France's continental nature 'repugna el abandono del suelo patrio' (181) and up to the time of Napoleon her wars were always 'encajadas en el criterio tradicional, formado por la lógica de la Historia' (180).

Ganivet's prescription follows logically from his diagnosis:

> nuestro criterio creo yo que debería ser tan rígido que rehuyera toda complicación en los asuntos continentales, aunque fuese para resolver los mayores conflictos de nuestra propia política; porque, por muy grandes que fueran los beneficios obtenidos, nunca llegarían a compensar las consecuencias perniciosas que por necesidad habrían de derivarse de un acto político contrario a la esencia de nuestro territorio (236).

Spain's aggressive role has lasted a long time, but it has still not ousted the fundamental, native spirit of independence, and this spirit of independence will inevitably assert itself again and must do so if the country is to prosper:

> el espíritu de agresión [. . .] no ha llegado a imponérsenos, y ha de tener su fin cuando se extingan los últimos ecos de la política que le dio origen (185-6).

Here, of course, Ganivet admits, and protests against, a breakdown in the cause-effect relationship that exists between the territorial spirit and the country's policy, in the same way that he admits a deviation of France's policy from her territorial spirit since the time of the Revolution, and in the same way that, in his *Epistolario*, he affirmed a departure of Germany's policy from her true native spirit under Bismarck (II, 964-5). But Ganivet's determinist approach to civilization does not therefore break down. If a country abandons its native course, he alleges, it is because of particular influences that have prevailed over the territorial spirit, and these particular influences have their own explanation and their own logic.[1] There is no need

---

[1] *Cf.* Non que cette loi [imposed by physical environment] s'accomplisse toujours jusqu'au bout; parfois des perturbations se rencontrent;

to review his arguments again. Briefly, Napoleon was an islander who imposed his own island aggression on France, and Spain's aggression was a metamorphosis of the spirit of independence, produced by regional rivalries (the spirit of independence again). Pages 180–7 offer ample evidence of the author's sustained determinism in dealing with these deviations from the territorial spirit. Where the territorial spirit fails to explain, 'la fuerza de los acontecimientos' (188), 'la fatalidad histórica' (222), takes over. But the territorial spirit cannot be suppressed for ever: 'la lógica de la Historia' demands that Spain should enter upon a period of true independence, with the concentration of national energies within national frontiers (225). It is Ganivet's aim in the *Idearium* to define for his readers the insistent demands of historical logic in the case of Spain, and thus to direct their energies towards the more efficient attainment of the inevitable.

Within this determinist pattern of Spanish civilization that Ganivet presents in *Idearium español*, what is the position of Christianity? It is clearly an important question for a proper understanding of the book, for Christianity in its alleged evolution from stoicism plays an important part in Spanish national character as interpreted by Ganivet. Most of the evidence for a discussion of the problem is to be found in the opening pages of the book, where the author traces the evolution of the Spanish religious spirit.

In accordance with his determinist approach and his insistence on the inevitable influence of national character

---

mais, quand il en est ainsi, ce n'est pas que la loi soit fausse, c'est qu'elle n'a pas seule agi. Des éléments nouveaux sont venus se mêler aux éléments anciens; de grandes forces étrangères sont venues contrarier les forces primitives (*HLA*, I, xxii).

H

on imported elements of civilization, Ganivet attacks imposed unity:

> Las unidades aparentes y convencionales no pueden destruir
> la diversidad real de las cosas: no sirven más que para en-
> cubrirla (168).

An absolute and universal Christian philosophy such as
the Scholastics sought to establish is harmful, and Ganivet
emphasizes the diversity of Christianity both as a fact in
the past and as a desirable aim in the future.[1] For during
the Middle Ages, through centuries of contacts and conflict with the Moslems, the Spanish religious spirit was
drawn away from the sterile and at times ridiculous debates of the Scholastics and found its true expression in
action, 'entre el chocar de las armas y el hervir de la
sangre', and thence in popular war poetry, 'nuestra *Summa*
teológica y filosófica' (160), 'cristiana y arábiga a la vez'
(161), which itself gave birth to the most notable tendencies of the Spanish religious spirit: mysticism and
fanaticism (161). Alongside the creations of this peculiarly
Spanish religious spirit, Ganivet maintains, doctrinal
writings in Spain seem inferior, a creation of the central-
izing, universal Church rather than of Spain's own
essential being.

But Ganivet's determinist view of Christianity is not

---

[1] Esa evolución, sin embargo, no fue igual ni pudo serlo en las diversas
provincias del Imperio romano [. . .]. Aun en aquellos países que
conservaron invariable lo fundamental de la religión, hubo diver-
gencias nacidas de la variedad de temperamentos y acentuadas gradual-
mente conforme los cambios históricos iban dando vida a nuevos
rasgos característicos y diferenciadores (157–8).
   Para que la filosofía cristiana no sea una fórmula convencional, para
que ejerza influencia real en la vida de los hombres, es preciso que
arranque de esa misma vida, como las leyes, como el arte [. . .]. Sería,
pues, muy fecundo y en ninguna manera peligroso romper la unidad
filosófica (166–70).

confined to emphasis on its inevitable geographical diversity. Christianity itself is presented as a product of historical factors, the outcome of religious and philosophical exhaustion:

> destruida la religión pagana por la filosofía y la filosofía por los filósofos, no quedaba más salida que una creencia que penetrase, no en forma de símbolos, venidos a la sazón muy a menos, sino en forma de rayo ideal, taladrando e incendiando (155–6).

It was necessary for Jesus to die, says Ganivet, in order that Christian doctrines should flourish: 'sin su sacrificio, Jesús hubiera sido un moralista más' (156), and without the Christian martyrs, 'el único medio eficaz de propaganda', 'el cristianismo hubiera sido una moral más, agregada a las muchas que han existido y existen sin ejercer visible influencia' (156). 'Todas las religiones, y en general todas las ideas, se han propagado y propagan y propagarán en igual forma: son como piedras que, cayendo en un estanque, producen un círculo de ondulaciones de varia amplitud y de mayor o menos persistencia' (156). It matters little that immediately after this Ganivet continues with the following image, which is so often quoted as evidence of his Christian faith:

> el cristianismo cayó desde muy alto, desde el [c]ielo, y por esta razón sus ondulaciones fueron tan amplias y duraderas (156).

This is surely no more than a sop to his readers;[1] it may even have been added at the suggestion of that person

---

[1] Thus, referring to the *Libro de Granada*, Ganivet wrote:
no quisiera perder la estimación de mi gente por exceso de celo, ya que mi carácter me condena a hacer cosas que van contra la corriente (NML, p. 103),
and, with reference to *El escultor de su alma*:
parece escrita por un creyente. Te digo esto no vayas a pensar que soy

who, he claims, saw the manuscript of the *Idearium* before
it went to press (II, 1066). At all events, in the next words
Ganivet presses again, with a characteristically determinist image, the 'naturalness' with which he believes
Christianity to have spread:

> porque ¿qué admiración puede causar que en diversos cam-
> pos simultáneamente labrados, abonados y sembrados de
> trigo, nazcan simultáneamente muchas, infinitas matas de
> trigo? (156).

For the determinist the only real cause of wonder might
be that Christianity established itself among such different
peoples, and Ganivet, consistent with his philosophy,
seeks out a 'natural' explanation for the fact. He attributes
it not to any divine power, but to 'hábiles injertos' via
stoicism (156–7). Where there is no such favourable state
of receptiveness, as in present-day primitive peoples, he
believes that Christianity can be established only by the
permanent action of a superior people. Left to themselves,
the natives of Africa would revert to their own crude
divinities (169). This view, says Ganivet, in an extremely
revealing paragraph, does not controvert the universality
and catholicity of the Christian religion, but such an un-
natural anomaly as the thorough and rapid conversion of
primitive peoples would require 'una causa excepcional,
extraordinaria' such as the 'estado de postración ideal a
que llegó el espíritu grecorromano' (170). Christianity,
then, is not its own exceptional cause for Ganivet, and
never has been; divine intervention plays no part in

---

tan estúpido que voy a poner en escena cosas contrarias al espíritu
local (NML, p. 108).

It should be noted also that the first edition of *Idearium español* (p. 10)
does not, like the Aguilar edition, have a capital *C* in *cielo*. See also below,
p. 129, n. 2.

Ganivet's thought, unless it be in God's own submission to the determinist pattern of life on earth and His wise choice of the most appropriate sowing time for the Christian faith.

It surely follows from the above that, despite the contrary claims of countless critics—many of them made, inexcusably, since the publication of Abad's fine article of 1925[1]—Ganivet is neither a true Catholic nor a true Christian. Nor are his views on religion merely 'confused'. They are extremely lucid and completely consistent with his basic determinism. And the *Epistolario* is there with its own abundant evidence, of which the following is merely a sample:

> Lo real es que toda la caterva de dioses ha salido de nuestro meollo, unos más divinos y otros más humanizados, el más humano Jesús; y lo real es que nosotros los occidentales a este nos agregamos por ser el último en el orden del tiempo y en el de la posibilidad (II, 975–6).[2]

Man needs faith, but as Ganivet points out in the *Idearium*, no new faith is forthcoming: 'la Humanidad hace ya

---

[1] C. Mª. Abad, 'Angel Ganivet', in *Razón y Fe* LXXII (May-August 1925), 18–30, 190–207. The following will serve as a pointer to Abad's finding:

> Está de sobra probado que Ganivet no cree en la divinidad del catolicismo, ni en la divinidad de Jesucristo; más aún, ni en la existencia de un Dios personal (op. cit., pp. 26–7).

[2] Letters not included in the *OC Epistolario* offer further evidence:

> Yo creo, sin embargo, que esa idea de Dios fue un medio de que se valieron los hombres, que siempre se odiaron cordialmente, para llenar los huecos de su ignorancia y para tener una autoridad a quien respetar y adorar fuera de ellos mismos [. . .]. Pero, aun siendo falso, es muy conveniente ese ídolo, como punto donde alguna vez se reunían las miradas de los hombres (In *Helios* I, 1903, 269).

For the rest, statements of the type 'Si hubiera tenido algunas creencias religiosas no estaría donde estoy' (cit. AGM, p. 107), 'Conste que yo no creo, ni quiero creer por ahora' (NML, p. 58), 'no me encuentro muy católico' (NML, p. 104) are frequent enough in Ganivet's letters to remove all doubt about his own lack of faith.

siglos que tiene seca la matriz y no puede engendrar
nuevos dioses' (168). He must cling, then, to what he has.
Ganivet, in his *Epistolario*, opposed Renan's attacks on
Christianity not because he considered them to be false,
but because by these attacks the French writer sought to
deprive his readers of a desirable ideal. 'Los sectarios
chillan contra la ignorancia que cierra los ojos a la verdad;
pero si no hubiera ignorancia y nos quedáramos todos con
la verdad solo, ¡valiente *juerga* nos esperaba!' (II, 826).
And so Christianity takes its all-important place in the
Idearium—not because Ganivet is a Christian, but because
he is a determinist and because he sees Christianity as a
fundamental element in Spanish civilization. Science, art
and religion, he affirms, are simply different ways of in-
terpreting reality, and a given nation will reveal itself best
in one way or another according to its character (209).[1]

---

[1] Suele pensarse que la religión es superior al arte y que el arte es
superior a la ciencia, considerando solo la elevación del objeto hacia
el cual tienden; pero, visto desde el punto de vista en que yo me coloco,
como fuerzas constituyentes del alma de un país, la superioridad
depende del carácter de cada país. En el fondo, ciencia, arte y religión
son una misma cosa: la ciencia interpreta la realidad mediante fórmulas,
el arte mediante imágenes y la religión mediante símbolos, y rara es la
obra humana en que se encuentra una interpretación pura [. . .]. La
diferencia real está en el sujeto; según la aptitud espiritual predominante
en cada individuo, el mundo se muestra en una u otra forma (209).
There is a remarkably similar passage in Taine:
Prenons d'abord les trois principales œuvres de l'intelligence humaine,
la religion, l'art, la philosophie. Qu'est-ce qu'une philosophie sinon
une conception de la nature et de ses causes primordiales, sous forme
d'abstractions et de formules? Qu'y a-t-il au fond d'une religion et
d'un art sinon une conception de cette même nature et de ces mêmes
causes primordiales, sous forme de symboles plus ou moins arrêtés et
de personnages plus ou moins précis, avec cette différence que dans
le premier cas on croit qu'ils existent, et dans le second qu'ils n'existent
pas? Que le lecteur considère quelques-unes de ces grandes créations
de l'esprit dans l'Inde, en Scandinavie, en Perse, à Rome, en Grèce, et
il verra que partout l'art est une sorte de philosophie devenue sensible,
la religion une sorte de poëme tenu pour vrai, la philosophie une sorte
d'art et de religion desséchée et réduite aux idées pures. Il y a donc au

The Spanish spirit is religious and artistic (212), and it is thus through religion and art that the Spanish spirit must continue to express itself. In the following lines Ganivet presses the case for religion:

> Cuanto en España se construya con carácter nacional debe estar sustentado sobre los sillares de la tradición. Eso es lo lógico y eso es lo noble, pues habiéndonos arruinado en la defensa del catolicismo, no cabría mayor afrenta que ser traidores para con nuestros padres y añadir a la tristeza de un vencimiento, acaso transitorio, la humillación de someternos a la influencia de las ideas de nuestros vencedores (172).

There is little joy in his case. It is but one of several passages in the *Idearium* in which, as in Taine's writings, determinism and stoicism come together: the stoic acceptance of what is fundamental and, thus, inevitable.

One cannot leave the question of determinism in *Idearium español* without considering Ganivet's attitude to art and literature. It has been touched on earlier in this chapter, but now it must be considered more critically. For art and literature are spheres of human activity in which one suspects that the individuality of the artist, so personal in its complexity, might lift itself beyond the simple forces and categories established by Ganivet. However, where the arts are mentioned in the *Idearium*, there is no evidence that Ganivet believes this to be the case. The following passage is characteristic of his approach:

> Si contrastamos el pensamiento filosófico de una obra maestra de arte con el pensamiento de la nación en que tuvo

---

centre de chacun de ces trois groupes un élément commun, la conception du monde et de son principe, et s'ils diffèrent entre eux, c'est que chacun combine avec l'élément commun, un élément distinct: ici la puissance d'abstraire, là la faculté de personnifier et de croire, là enfin le talent de personnifier sans croire (*HLA*, I, xxxv–xxxvi).

origen, veremos que, con independencia del propósito del
autor, la obra encierra un sentido que pudiera llamarse
histórico, concordante con la historia nacional, una interpretación del espíritu de esta historia. Y cuanto más
estrecha sea la concordancia, el mérito de la obra será
mayor, porque el artista saca sus fuerzas invisiblemente de la
confusión de sus ideas con las ideas de su territorio, obrando
como un reflector en el que estas ideas se cruzan y se
mezclan y adquieren, al cruzarse y mezclarse, la luz de que
separadas carecían (278).[1]

Thereupon he proceeds to show how in *La vida es sueño*
Calderón 'nos da [. . .] una explicación clara, lúcida y
profética de nuestra historia' (278). In similar fashion,
Velázquez and Goya and Lope de Vega and the author of
the *Celestina* are seen to exemplify the fundamental
Spanish spirit of independence (212–16). And Seneca, he
says, simply gave expression to the stoicism he found
around him, 'obrando como obran los verdaderos hombres de genio' (152). And the *Romancero* contains Spain's
'*Summa* teológica y filosófica' (160). And the mysticism
and fanaticism born of the Reconquest found expression
both in the mystics and in the *autos de fe* (161). And we
have seen how Cervantes and the *Quijote* are repeatedly
invoked by Ganivet for the light they throw on fundamental Spanish character: Cervantes was the greatest of
the *conquistadores*, the *Quijote* is 'nuestra obra típica', and

---

[1] En cela consiste l'importance des œuvres littéraires; elles sont in-
structives, parce qu'elles sont belles; leur utilité croît avec leur per-
fection; et si elles fournissent des documents, c'est qu'elles sont des
monuments. Plus un livre rend les sentiments visibles, plus il est
littéraire; car l'office propre de la littérature, est de noter les sentiments. Plus un livre note des sentiments importants, plus il est placé
haut dans la littérature [. . .]. C'est donc principalement par l'étude des
littératures que l'on pourra faire l'histoire morale et marcher vers la
connaissance des lois psychologiques, d'où dépendent les événements
(*HLA*, I, xlvi–xlviii).

the Manchegan knight represents the characteristic
Spanish attitude to justice.

> Todos los pueblos tienen un tipo real o imaginario en quien
> encarnan sus propias cualidades; en todas las literaturas en-
> contraremos una obra maestra en la que ese hombre típico
> figura entrar en acción, ponerse en contacto con la sociedad
> de su tiempo y atravesar una larga serie de pruebas donde se
> aquilata el temple de su espíritu, que es el espíritu propio de
> su raza (303).

It is Don Quixote who fulfils this role in Spain, like
Ulysses in Greece, like Robinson Crusoe in England, like
Dante in Italy, like Faust in Germany.

Now these claims by Ganivet, based on the unproven
assumption that what is great is representative may or
may not be justified. That is not our present concern. Far
more important for an understanding of his determinism
is the fact that he invokes authors and works only for
their documentary value, for the evidence he can find in
them to support his own particular view of the Spanish
national spirit. If there are other aspects to the authors and
works he cites, they are allowed no place in the *Idearium*.
There is no question of a dispassionate, unprejudiced
approach to a work of literature to see what it itself
suggests as an artistic whole. In the same way that Neo-
grammarians of the age were ransacking early texts for
confirmation of their inadequately based and over-
simplified theories of linguistic change, so Ganivet ran-
sacks Spanish art and literature for evidence of his
grotesquely simple, determinist view of Spanish civilization. He admits nothing that can offend the purity of
his ideal vision.

And here we have touched on a key word for an

understanding of Ganivet: ideal. Occasionally as a noun, usually as an adjective, the word *ideal* appears more than fifty times in the one hundred and fifty-five pages of the book, backed up strongly by closely associated words such as *idea, ideología, idealiza, idealmente* and, in the title of the work, *idearium*. Used by Ganivet in an apparently straightforward, untendentious way, *ideal* means 'pertaining to ideas'. Thus, when the author writes of Spain's 'mendicidad ideal' he is referring to the nation's 'falta de ideas' and he places it beside 'mendicidad económica' as something to be remedied (283). Similarly, he contrasts 'acción ideal' with 'acción por medio de la fuerza' (225), 'fuerza ideal' with 'fuerzas materiales' (266), 'creación ideal' with 'dominación material' (304). But the lines that follow immediately upon the last example point to an important restriction of meaning:

> Nuestro espíritu parece tosco, porque está embastecido por luchas brutales; parece flaco, porque está solo nutrido de ideas ridículas, copiadas sin discernimiento; y parece poco original, porque ha perdido la audacia, la fe en sus propias ideas, porque busca fuera de sí lo que dentro de sí tiene (304-5).

Here Ganivet is not simply advocating a revival of Spain's mental and intellectual life; he is calling for intellectual regeneration in a particular direction: in accordance with certain ideas and with the rejection of others. And, of course, there is a similar restriction of meaning in the first section of the book, where he claims that the most profound moral and religious element in Spain's 'constitución ideal' is stoicism and that this reveals itself 'en cuanto se ahonda un poco en la superficie o corteza ideal de nuestra nación' (151-2), and when he affirms that the territorial spirit of independence is at the centre of the nation's 'evolución ideal' (175–6). In all these cases *ideal* clearly means 'reduced to the essential schema that Ganivet himself finds in Spanish civilization'. But this 'essential schema' is not purely conceptual; the word *ideal* has not only undergone a restriction of meaning; it has also undergone an extension of meaning, and become the emotion-charged bearer of a vast cultural complexity. Now 'la idea romana' can be identified with 'la fuerza', and 'la idea cristiana' with 'el amor' (201–2).[1] And Christianity can be shown escaping from mere reason and philosophy and penetrating 'en forma de rayo ideal, taladrando e incendiando' (156). And the whole train of desirable 'engrandecimiento ideal' (222), 'fuerza ideal' (266), 'fuego ideal' (301), 'renacimiento ideal' (302) and 'nuestro gran triunfo ideal' (303) is wide open. It is 'ideas' that really live (221), that are important (262), that guide and sustain (266), that continue to flourish when the mere political power of force has passed away (282):

si por el solo esfuerzo de nuestra inteligencia lográsemos reconstituir la unión familiar de todos los pueblos his-pánicos e infundir en ellos el culto de unos mismos ideales, de nuestros ideales, cumpliríamos una gran misión histórica (282).

[1] Compare Ganivet's use of the word *idea* in the following passages: La exaltación del espíritu religioso, la veneración a los reyes, la caba-llerosidad y la galantería, la lucha por la fe y por la patria, son las ideas que laten en esos cantares y romances, síntesis en que a veces se con-funden la vida subjetiva y objetiva y de la que pudiera pacientemente sacarse todo un sistema de filosofía moral, demostrándose de esta suerte que, aun en los periodos en que la ignorancia sea mayor, pueden conservar los pueblos profundamente arraigadas esas ideas fundamen-tales que son como las piedras angulares del edificio de la vida (*España filosófica contemporánea*, II, 603).
La idea en que se ampara la fuerza de Europa es el cristianismo, una idea de paz y de amor, que por esto no pudo nacer entre nosotros (*El porvenir de España*, II, 1068).

No wonder Ganivet takes Don Quixote as a guide:

> y su acción [let us say rather, for Ganivet, 'su pensamiento']
> es una inacabable creación, un prodigio humano, en el que
> se idealiza todo cuanto en la realidad existe (304).

Ganivet, like Don Quixote, detests the impurities of the
material world. And there, as further evidence, are the
words that he sets up in distasteful opposition to his ideal
realm: *experimental, práctico, realista, vulgar*. The *ideal* is the
all-important realm of purity; the rest is impure and of no
real value. Thus, since Bacon, says Ganivet, men have
striven to establish empirical methods and empirical
knowledge, 'una ciencia puramente realista y práctica',
and their works have perhaps been useful on the material
plane, offering us certain practical advantages 'como el
poder viajar de prisa, aunque por desgracia sea para llegar
a donde lo mismo se llegaría viajando despacio'. 'Pero su
valor ideal es nulo,' he continues, 'y en vez de destronar a
la metafísica, han venido a servirla y hasta quizá a favore-
cerla' (165). Thereupon, he recalls the episode of his
umbrella and the thoughtfulness of his Flemish maid: he
himself, he says, had acted in accordance with 'la fuerza
perenne del ideal'; the maid had been guided by '[la]
ciencia experimental y práctica'. One must be grateful to
such prudent and practical people, the author continues,
'pero digo también que cuando acierto a levantarme
siquiera dos palmos sobre las vulgaridades rutinarias que
me rodean y siento el calor y la luz de alguna idea grande y
pura, todas esas bellas invenciones [telescope, microscope,
railway, etc.] no me sirven para nada' (165–6).[1]

---

[1] Laín Entralgo's objection to this passage is obviously justified and
necessary:
> Cuando [Ganivet] afirma que con los inventos técnicos se camina más
> de prisa que sin ellos, pero se llega al mismo sitio, uno adivina la

Cherished 'ideas' and despised reality. The contrast is pressed again and again. But is not Spanish civilization itself a reality? In the search for the all-important 'fuerza dominante y céntrica' in which the ideal of Spain is to be found, has not Ganivet's longing for a pure realm of 'ideas' caused him to seize too hastily upon characteristics that are perhaps not really fundamental? Does his case for stoicism stand the test of the reality he despises? Can his case for the territorial spirit stand up to the probings of those practical, realistic 'hombres sabios y prudentes' whom he treats with such noble condescension (165–6)? These questions become especially urgent when one considers the following passage, in which I find the key to Ganivet's whole approach to his subject:

las ideas que nos vienen al espíritu cuando vemos una nave flotando sobre las aguas son las que más claramente revelan nuestra concepción universal y armónica de la vida. Yo vivo en una casa rodeada de árboles, junto al mar. A veces veo en el lejano horizonte la forma indecisa de un barco que surge entre el mar y el cielo, como portador de mensajeros espirituales; después comienzo a distinguir el velamen y la arboladura; luego el casco y algo confuso que se mueve; más cerca, las maniobras de los tripulantes; por fin, veo entrar el barco en el puerto y arrojar por las escotillas, sobre el muelle, la carga multiforme que lleva escondida en su

sentencia resignada y calmosa del arriero andaluz, viendo junto a su recua, a la cruda luz de la carretera serrana, la rápida marcha del automóvil moderno. Aparte, naturalmente, el desconocimiento del problema: averiguar, mediante la técnica física, la composición elemental de una estrella, seguir la órbita de un electrón o extirpar un tumor cerebral, no es caminar más de prisa, sino 'llegar a otro sitio'. El mismo sentimiento de dolorida resignación y cínico casticismo surge luego al sentar con triste jactancia—¡en vísperas del 98!—'que la habanera por sí sola vale por toda la producción de los Estados Unidos, sin excluir la de máquinas de coser y aparatos telefónicos' (in *Ensayos y Estudios*, II, 1940, 69–70).

enorme buche. Y pienso que así se nos presentan también las ideas; las cuales comienzan por un destello divino que, conforme toma cuerpo en la realidad, va perdiendo su originaria pureza hasta hundirse y encenagarse y envilecerse en las más groseras encarnaciones. Por un instante que el alma se deleite en la contemplación de una idea que nace limpia y sin mancha entre las espumas del pensamiento, ¡cuánta angustia después para hacer sensible esa idea en algunas de las menguadas y raquíticas formas de que nuestro escaso poder dispone!, ¡cuánta tristeza al verla convertida en algo material, manchada por la impureza inseparable de lo material! (199–200).

First, while reality is still at a distance, the 'destello divino', the 'idea que nace limpia y sin mancha entre las espumas del pensamiento'; then, with its approach, 'las más groseras encarnaciones', 'la impureza inseparable de lo material'. Transposed into terms of Spanish civilization, the image becomes immediately and obviously relevant to the question of Ganivet's approach: on the one hand, Spanish civilization contemplated from the un-sullied realm of thought and feeling, free from the impurities of real-life contact, and, on the other, Spanish civilization in all its despairing variety and complexity, recalcitrant to facile generalizations and pseudo-intellectual daydreams. There can be no doubt about where Ganivet takes his stand. For there is, in the *Idearium*, no evidence of extensive documentation, no evidence of empirical reconstruction from masses of facts, no evidence of that interplay between facts and theory that scholars as different as E. H. Carr and Karl Popper have considered to be the *sine qua non* of all responsible historical study. For Ganivet 'purely objective observations' yield up only the 'external mechanism', the 'wrappings' (174–5). He is impatient with the 'impureza inseparable de lo material' and he despises the realistic, experimental, practical approach to knowledge. He is driven on, in his studies as in his daily life, by the 'fuerza perenne del ideal' (166). And so, despite his view of civilization as an organism of interdependent parts and despite his use of evolutionist and psychological terminology, in fact Ganivet scorns the naturalist's and psychologist's submission to observed facts. Hence my earlier expression, 'biological *pretence*', for Ganivet's own prime aim is not to observe but to interpret, not to study but to explain. With the facile assurance of a café *raconteur*—and with a similar disregard for facts—Ganivet places himself triumphantly, with a single bound, at the 'ideal' centre of his subject and thereupon proceeds to select, from the limitless complexity of Spanish civilization, a number of facts that appear to support his view, and to present unavoidable contrary evidence as signs of a deviation from the nation's proper path. It is the point at which Ganivet's various uses of the word *ideal* come together and are seen in their proper perspective: *ideal*, pertaining to the idea; *ideal*, pertaining to the essence; *ideal*, pertaining to the desirable. What Ganivet conceives 'limpia y sin mancha entre las espumas del pensamiento' (with both restriction and extension of the term *idea*) is projected outwards on to Spain and presented to us as the essence of Spanish civilization, 'un ideal bien cimentado' (258) after which Spaniards must strive. Consequently, my attempt to separate these different meanings was artificial: 'mendicidad ideal' refers not simply to the nation's lack of ideas; it refers also—and principally—to the general failure to recognize and act in accordance with those forces that Ganivet feels constitute the essential basis of Spanish civilization.

But how does so much 'idealism' fit into the pattern of Ganivet's determinism? To understand this, one must consider briefly the view of history that Ganivet deplores: the 'criterio excesivamente positivista' of late-nineteenth-century historical studies, with their total submission to facts (224). The important thing, says Ganivet, is not to pile up facts in meaningless profusion, but to see their connection with one another and with the spirit of the country to which they belong:

> lo esencial en la historia es el ligamen de los hechos con el espíritu del país donde han tenido lugar; solo a este precio se puede escribir una historia verdadera, lógica y útil. ¿A qué puede conducir una serie de hechos exactos y apoyados en pruebas fehacientes si se da a todos estos hechos igual valor, si se los presenta con el mismo relieve y no se marca cuáles son concordantes con el carácter de la nación, cuáles son opuestos, cuáles son favorables y cuáles contrarios a la evolución natural de cada territorio, considerado con sus habitantes como una personalidad histórica? (224).

But Ganivet's view of positivism is too narrow. Positivism was the prevailing characteristic in Western thought during the second half of the nineteenth century and the *Idearium* bears clearly the stamp of its age. For positivism included not merely the amassing of facts; it included also the framing of laws.[1] And historical studies of the age represent the whole range of possibilities: from the patient, scholarly master of detail, who compiled great stores of facts from archaeological remains, inscriptions,

---

[1] José Martínez Ruiz (Azorín) realized this when he wrote, in 1897: Hamon es un obrero intelectual de una laboriosidad extraordinaria; positivista convencido, trabaja *sobre los hechos*, y de ellos saca todas sus conclusiones, y por ellos formula la *ley*, la regla media, general, que rige y gobierna las relaciones sociales (*OC* I, 2nd ed., Madrid 1959, 286; Martínez Ruiz's italics).

cartularies, government reports, etc.—and perhaps never arrived at a synthesis—to the hasty enthusiast, impatient with mere 'fact-grubbing', who sought to discover a pattern of causal relationship within his own scant store of hastily garnered and perhaps inadequately founded observations. The great scholars of the time are less extreme, but the difference between them is clear: on the one hand, the formidable solidity of Mommsen and Maitland; on the other, the super-historical 'sociology' of Auguste Comte and the ambitious studies of history and literature by Hippolyte Taine.[1]

Ganivet's own extreme position is evident. Like Taine in France, so Ganivet in Spain is the 'metaphysician of positivism', and with far less concern than the French thinker for the facts of civilization. 'Toute mon ambition est d'écrire mon idée,' wrote Taine; to which a critic has retorted: 'So much does dogma dominate. He is caught in the tyranny of his own intuitive way of thinking; *a priori* system determines each separate judgement, controls the point of view, and so shapes or mis-shapes the facts themselves.'[2] And what is here said of Taine's treatment of civilizations can be said with greater justification of Ganivet's far less documented and far less subtle treatment of Spanish civilization in *Idearium español*. For he is the Don Quixote of positivism, the idealist who projects everything from within him, from the inner realm of the pure 'idea'. It is for this reason that I have preferred the word determinism to describe his work. Of the positivist aim to discover facts and establish causal relationships, almost only the second part remains. Ganivet regards the

[1] R. G. Collingwood, *The Idea of History*, Oxford University Press, 1961, pp. 126–33.
[2] H. B. Charlton, in his preface to Taine's *Introduction à l'histoire de la littérature anglaise*, Manchester University Press, 1936, p. 6.

world of facts as unworthy; 'lo que realmente vive son las ideas' (221).

But these 'ideas', this ideal realm in which Ganivet takes such manifest delight in the *Idearium*, is it a purely capricious and arbitrary invention? We have found very little to recommend it as a valid interpretation of Spanish civilization. One lacks the evidence that a more prosaic, more empirical approach would give, and one regrets the absence of logical discipline in the organization of the scanty evidence that is presented. We are in the realm of the 'idea que nace limpia y sin mancha entre las espumas del pensamiento' (199). But where does that 'idea' come from? If it bears little relationship to the realities of Spanish civilization, does it perhaps bear a more significant relationship to Ganivet's own inner world? Is the *Idearium* a study of Spain or is it a spiritual autobiography? In my next chapter I shall attempt to show that it is the latter.

V

IDEARIUM ESPAÑOL
AS A SPIRITUAL AUTOBIOGRAPHY

In this chapter I aim to show that Ganivet interprets the problem of Spain in terms of his own personal problem: that the aboulia he finds in Spain is his own aboulia, that the alleged 'fuerzas constituyentes' of Spain are his own 'fuerzas constituyentes', and that his prescription for national cure follows logically from his own self-probing.

Of course, for the more naïve determinist there is a ready explanation of such parallels that I must seek to discount: the man of genius, it is said, reflects what he finds around him; if there are parallels between Ganivet's own emotional state and that of his country as he describes it in the *Idearium*, it is because his own state reflects Spain's; Ganivet simply gave expression to the crisis of the age in which he lived (cf. *Idearium* 152, 278; and above, pp. 113–15). Indeed, if we omit the word 'simply', we cannot object completely to this view, for no man escapes entirely the influences of his age, and Ganivet, in his anguished search for an object of faith, is characteristic of many intellectuals of his day. But there is a long step from admitting this to accepting Ganivet's emotional state as the microcosm of Spain's ('una reducción fotográfica de la sociedad', 288). The determinist makes insufficient allowance for the individual and the artist, generalizing too easily from the individual to a class and from a class to a whole nation. To accept, as Ganivet does, that the degree of merit of a writer is in direct relation to the faithfulness

with which he reflects the spirit of his country's history
(278) and at the same time to uphold Ganivet as the microcosm of that spirit is to reject as inferior all other Spanish
writers of the age merely because their view of reality is
different from Ganivet's. But a writer does not simply
reflect: he selects and interprets and, outside the limited
realm of purely empirical study, seeks to justify his
own prejudices and obsessions with data taken from—or
dreamed into—the world of reality around him. And if his
prejudices and obsessions are characteristic of his age or
of his country or of his class, the particular combination
he makes of them is still his own. This is notably the case
with Ganivet. Nor is it simply a question of doubtful
selection or doubtful emphasis in the handling of a vast
store of information. Ganivet uses reality like a creative
writer: he does not merely reflect it; he seeks to re-create it.
In the present chapter I shall show the essentially personal
basis of this re-creation; in the following chapter I shall
consider some of the principal means by which Ganivet
communicates his re-creation of reality to his reader.

THE UNDERLYING ABOULIA

The basic malady of Spain, says Ganivet, is aboulia, 'extinción o debilitación grave de la voluntad' (286). In a less
chronic form, he believes, the malady is known to all of us:

> Hay una forma vulgar de la abulia que todos conocemos y a
> veces padecemos. ¿A quién no le habrá invadido en alguna
> ocasión esa perplejidad del espíritu, nacida del quebranto de
> fuerzas o del aplanamiento consiguiente a una inacción pro-
> longada, en que la voluntad, falta de idea dominante que la
> mueva, vacilante entre motivos opuestos que se contrabalan-
> cean, o dominada por una idea abstracta, irrealizable, per-

manece irresoluta, sin saber qué hacer y sin determinarse a hacer nada? Cuando tal situación de pasajera se convierte en crónica, constituye la abulia, la cual se muestra al exterior en la repugnancia de la voluntad a ejecutar actos libres (286–7).

To Ganivet, certainly, this 'perplejidad del espíritu' was well known and he probes it frequently in letters to his friends. 'Cada día,' he writes in the first letter of his *Epistolario* (18 February 1893), 'me va siendo más difícil concretar mis ideas y fijar mi pensamiento sobre un objeto determinado' (II, 811). Lacking the 'instrucción compacta' of either seminary or Institución Libre (II, 813; cf. above, 'la voluntad falta de una idea dominante que la mueva'), Ganivet finds the world around him aimless and repugnant, and is unable to assimilate its data. 'En tal estado,' he says, 'el espíritu se va [. . . pero . . .] el espíritu que abandonó la realidad por demasiado baja no puede elevarse a la infinitud por demasiado alta' (II, 811–12; cf. above, 'la voluntad . . ., dominada por una idea abstracta, irrealizable'). The outcome is inaction: 'la vida retrograda, no pudiendo vencer la pereza, que le impide continuar asimilándose elementos nuevos para renovar la vida al compás del tiempo' (II, 812; cf. 'el entendimiento parece como que se petrifica y se incapacita para la asimilación de ideas nuevas', 287). As in the *Idearium* so also in this letter, Ganivet diagnoses the malady as 'la *abulia* o debilitación de la voluntad' (II, 812). Spain's alleged illness, then, is clearly Ganivet's own.

We have seen the explanation that might occur to the more naïve determinist: Ganivet simply experienced and gave expression to the aboulia of the Spanish people as a whole. To disprove this, it is necessary to make a large detour and indicate the essentially personal nature of

Ganivet's own aboulia. It arose, I believe, from two principal causes that cannot be considered common to the whole Spanish nation or even to a major part of it: lack of religious faith and disillusion with science. Ganivet's writings from 1888 to 1896 offer ample evidence.

'Los individuos y las colectividades obran guiados por una idea directiva' (II, 579-80). In these words, from the beginning of *España filosófica contemporánea*, I find the principal *leit-motiv* of Ganivet's writings and the key to his intellectual and emotional development. Man, says Ganivet, needs guidance, an ideal, a touchstone of faith, something positive to give aim to his existence; without such guidance he is torn between contradictory tendencies, becomes sceptical about the various possibilities available to him, and sinks into apathy. But where can man find such guidance? In his thesis Ganivet noted only two fields of faith, and thence also, of enthusiasm and activity, in the Spain of his day: that of religion and that of science and empirical study, 'el espiritualismo y el materialismo' (II, 592-6, 662). For the rest, he found everywhere apathy, indifference, lack of direction, lack of ideals and, underlying it all, scepticism, 'el escepticismo, que nada afirma ni nada niega, que priva a la inteligencia de la seguridad o fijeza en el conocimiento y a la voluntad de la convicción y la firmeza en sus determinaciones' (II, 586). Four years later, in the letter referred to above, he made the point again:

En el fondo, muchos de los hombres nuevos son un poco 'abúlicos', con excepción de los que reciben instrucción compacta, sea en seminarios, sea en la compañía de la Institución Libre, etcétera (II, 813).

Religion and empirical study, then, are two possible fields of faith for Ganivet himself. But in his first doctorate thesis he did not take sides and his work ended on the threshold of conflict between them. For an understanding of his own attitude one must consider the evidence of his other writings, and especially of his letters to friends.

In none of these writings have I found evidence of religious faith. On the other hand, I have found ample evidence of lack of faith (cf. above, pp. 107–13) and I share Castro Villacañas' view that Ganivet had lost any religious faith he ever possessed before he moved to Madrid in 1888.[1] Gods and religions, he affirms, are man-made creations and the significance of Christ is primarily geographical. We accept him in the West because he is chronologically the most recent of the gods and because he is the most human,[2] but it is we ourselves whom we see as the real gods today and, because we find ourselves inadequate for the role, we despair (II, 975–6). But man needs faith in something beyond himself and it is therefore wrong to destroy the results of nineteen centuries of labour and fatigue, as Renan tried to do; one can deny religion all positive value and nevertheless admit completely its 'ideal' sense, in the same way that one can admit the 'ideal' significance of Jupiter and Venus though originally the one may have been simply a tribal chief and the other a primitive prostitute. Besides, continues Ganivet, a fine position we should be in if we all had to live solely with the truth! (II, 825–7). The outcome of all this is that Ganivet, 'sin ser católico' and convinced that Catholicism in another two or three hundred years will be a mere historical memory, nevertheless sides firmly

[1] 'Notas para un centenario: [3] Hombre sin fe', in *Arriba*, 7 March 1965.
[2] In the first edition of the *Epistolario* pronouns referring to Christ are not written with an initial capital letter. Contrast the Aguilar edition and see above, p. 110, n.

with the intransigents, those who defend the Catholic faith with exaggeration but also with enthusiasm, against the diplomats of the Church who spend their energies in political manoeuvrings (II, 1005–07). Without himself finding any apparent consolation in religion, Ganivet accepts it as a desirable aid to human existence.

In his attitude to religion I find no change during the period under review; in his attitude to science, on the other hand, I find optimism evolving to scepticism and positive distaste. Thus, in *España filosófica contemporánea* Ganivet emphasized the attraction of the scientist's great ideals, and in his second doctorate thesis, *Importancia de la lengua sánscrita*, he himself explored a sphere of positivist study and apparently found in it something of the thrill which he had said characterized such work. The new linguistics, he declared, demands 'un espíritu paciente y dispuesto para el análisis y una gran imparcialidad' (I, 893); its methods are those of the natural sciences, 'el análisis y la observación' (I, 894), and only by accepting as its basis 'el estudio analítico, comparativo e histórico de las lenguas' has linguistics acquired truly scientific solidity (I, 894). He concluded with warm praise for the sureness and solidity of Diez's work in the Romance field, and lamented the lack of individual initiative and official protection necessary for Spain to play her part in such studies. Thereafter, his enthusiasm for empirical study wanes. Like Faust before him, Ganivet discovers that empirical study can give him only the 'worms' of knowledge and not the great synthesis that he longs for:

Todos los sabios se esforzaron por mirar las cosas de cerca para conocerlas mejor; hoy no sólo se acercan, sino que descomponen, desmenuzan y luego miran con el microscopio. Sus juicios son necedades. Sus escritos igualarán con el tiempo en importancia a los que tú conservas en tu Archivo. Se conoce, no analizando, sino abstrayendo; cuanto es mejor la abstracción es mayor la distancia entre la inteligencia y la realidad, y el juicio es más exacto, más sereno. He aquí un argumento en pro de la Metafísica que no he leído en ningún metafísico (29 December 1891; in *Helios* III, 1904, 167).

Moreover, empirical study, he finds, undermines his confidence and kills his enthusiasm by pressing upon him its own transitory nature:

> Es preciso tener fe en la ciencia, en una ciencia, puesto que hay muchas y muchas tendencias y los hechos positivos nos quitan el entusiasmo demostrándonos que quizá lo que hoy priva—la ciencia experimental—sea mañana una obra más muerta que lo es hoy el escolasticismo o la retórica clásica. Veamos, pues, dónde hay que refugiarse para vivir lo más decente y filosóficamente posible (17 November 1893; II, 926).

As the last lines suggest, this is no mere intellectual development; it is also—and principally—emotional. Ganivet's growing disillusion with science and empirical study forms part of a far wider and growing disgust with the whole material world around him, and the process can be traced clearly in his letters to friends. He feels increasingly out of harmony with the world of reality, increasingly disgusted with people and their institutions ('imbéciles', 'estúpida canalla', 'tonterías', 'majaderías', 'ridiculeces') and, beyond this, increasingly obsessed with the emptiness and pointlessness of life in general ('el vacío de la vida en general', the lack of 'fines propios del hombre', the notion of 'la máquina de nuestra especie a la que vamos uncidos como esclavos', II, 1013–14).[1] The

---

[1] I have examined this development more fully in an article to be published shortly: 'From Reality to the Ideal in Ganivet's *Epistolario*'.

outcome is that state of *'abulia* o debilitación de la voluntad' whose essentially intimate, personal origin I have been
seeking to demonstrate, the malady that Ganivet diagnoses both in himself (in his *Epistolario*) and in Spain (in
Idearium español).

'FUERZAS CONSTITUYENTES'

Lacking faith in religion and disillusioned with empirical
study, Ganivet is obsessed with the notion of life's ultimate pointlessness. 'Veamos, pues, dónde hay que refugiarse para vivir lo más decente y filosóficamente posible'
(II, 926). The letter from which these words are taken
ends at this point, but Ganivet's own response, I suggest,
is implicit in his wording of the problem: one must withdraw from involvement with others ('refugiarse') and one
must adopt a philosophic attitude to life's misfortunes
('vivir lo más decente y filosóficamente posible'). The rest
of the *Epistolario* is there with its own impressive store of
evidence, and illustrates clearly both Ganivet's emphasis
on withdrawal:

> Cuando se desea la apacibilidad del espíritu necesaria para
> los trabajos y no se encuentra en la vida de sociedad, porque
> el carácter se ha torcido, se ha agriado y con su influencia
> echa a perder cuanto toca (que esto es más justo que creer
> que la culpa es de los *otros*, aun siendo estos otros unos
> solemnes *imbéciles*), hay siempre un recurso supremo: *ais-
> larse, rodeándose* de las cosas que tienen la virtud de calmar
> el espíritu (18 January 1894; II, 949–50),

and his advocacy of a stoic attitude to life's misfortunes:

> Las consecuencias de este modo de ver son las de la moral
> panteísta o las de la moral estoica, sin meterse en dibujos

[. . .]. Por vía de distracción, venga todo en buen hora, pero nada vale la pena de molestarse (4 January 1895; II, 1014–1016).

And, of course, the duality of stoicism and withdrawal from social involvement that Ganivet here accepts for himself recalls forcibly the duality of stoicism and independence (that is, withdrawal from international involvement) that in the *Idearium* he emphasizes in his treatment of Spain. Thus, to consider first the question of withdrawal, I find clear similarities between what he urges on a personal plane (in the *Epistolario*):

Supuesto que nos disguste el roce humano que hoy se gasta, ¿no es obra de prudencia disminuirlo y de resolución concluir con él? Yo creo que sí, y que en esto no hay flojedad ni egoísmo (17 November 1893; II, 923),

Quizá el placer que se busca en vencer se encontraría retirándose. No es que yo me haga apóstol de la gandulería, pues se puede ser enérgico y activo en mil cosas que no se oponen a ningún hecho natural ni producen colisión de ningún género (14 August 1894; II, 986),

and what he urges on a national plane (in the *Idearium*):

nuestra política territorial es la del retraimiento voluntario, el cual, si ya no fuera en sí tan lógico como es, habría de ser aceptado por decoro (235),

ya hay quien desea volver a las antiguas complicaciones, en vez de trabajar por aumentar la escasa fuerza motriz de que hoy disponemos. De aquí la necesidad perentoria de destruir las ilusiones nacionales; y el destruirlas no es obra de desesperados, es obra de noble y legítima ambición, por la cual comenzamos a fundar nuestro positivo engrandecimiento (271).

Nor does the similarity lie only in the advocacy of withdrawal from external involvements; the cause and the aim of that withdrawal, too, are basically the same: the cause, a sense of failure in external relationships ('lo general es que todos formen mal concepto [de mí . . .]. Aquí, ahora, en la última tanda de personas que he tenido que tratar, he quedado mal con el noventa y cinco por ciento', II, 993; cf. the failure of Spain's foreign policy), and the aim, a desire to find in withdrawal an honourable and decorous solution to that failure (cf. above: 'prudencia', 'no hay flojedad ni egoísmo'; 'decoro', 'noble y legítima ambición').

But here, it seems, we have passed from one 'fuerza constituyente' to another, from withdrawal to stoicism, for both on the personal plane and on the national plane the aim behind withdrawal would appear to be the stoic aim of dignity and decorum in face of misfortune. Indeed, Ganivet himself brings the two planes, personal and national, together in the opening pages of the *Idearium*, where he emphasizes the importance of stoicism in Spain's 'ideal constitution' and refers also to the impact on him of his own student reading of Seneca (152–3). The suggestion is that this gave form to something that he already felt, obscurely, within himself. Moreover, there is abundant biographical evidence of Ganivet's own stoicism in adversity: his determination, as a child and as a student, to overcome infirmity;[1] his concealment of suffering, even from his most intimate friends;[2] his view of sadness as a

---

[1] Recall, for example, his determination and his efforts to walk again, without crutches, after a serious fracture of the leg that prompted a pessimistic prognosis from his doctors (NML, Prologue to *Cartas finlandesas*, pp. xliii–xliv; Colombine, 'Angel Ganivet' [An interview with Ganivet's sister, Josefa], in *Heraldo de Madrid*, 28 January 1921), and his refusal to allow illness to interfere with his timetable of study and examinations (NML, op. cit., p. xliv).

[2] Thus, Nicolás María López refers to 'pasiones y contrariedades que

weakness and of compassion as a humiliation;[1] his notion
of suicide as an ultimate, dignified withdrawal if reality
should prove too oppressive. . . .[2] And now note Ganivet's view of himself: 'Sin vanidad aseguro que no hay dos
tan resistentes como yo para mantenerse tiesos en y contra la sociedad'.[3] And this view is echoed by his most
intimate friends, Nicolás María López:

La característica moral de su persona fue el dominio absoluto
que tenía sobre sí (NML, p. 14),

and Francisco Navarro Ledesma:

La valentía de su corazón, al cual nunca vi abatido, ni
siquiera cuando se hallaba en trances de muerte, era in-
domable (in *Los Lunes de El Imparcial*, 13 February 1899).

Finally, in case still further evidence should be required,
there are the works themselves, with their basically stoic
leit-motiv as defined by three of Ganivet's most authori-
tative critics:

La varia condición literaria de las obras de Ganivet—prosa
y verso, acción dramática y pasión lírica, humor y medita-

[Ganivet] siempre guardó en secreto' (NML, p. 8), and later comments:
Hay, indudablemente, en la vida de Ganivet, un fondo de misterio, de
dolor y silencio tan hermético, que ni a Navarro ni a mí, que fuimos
sus más íntimos confidentes, nos reveló jamás (NML, p. 34).
Thereafter, López compares his friend to Pío Cid, observing:
Todas las tristezas y amarguras atormentaron su espíritu, y nadie supo
nada de esto. Si alguna vez la queja asoma a sus labios, es con la
ironía profunda del sabio, o con la suprema resignación del santo o del
mártir (ibid).
[1] jamás se quejó ni se lamentó de nada [. . .]. Su amor propio le hacía
ocultar sus preocupaciones y tristezas, como si fueran delitos. Si
alguien le hubiera manifestado compasión, se hubiera sentido aver-
gonzado u ofendido (NML, *Viajes románticos de Antón del Sauce*,
Granada [1932?], pp. 28–9).
[2] [Ganivet] siempre tuvo y en repetidas ocasiones indicó [. . .] el
propósito de morirse *cuando quisiera* (F. Navarro Ledesma, Prologue to
Epistolario, 1904, p. 19).
[3] 25 April 1896; in *Helios* II (1903), 550.

ción—se resuelve en una idea superior y constante, permanente a través de los más confusos momentos, si bien
mude en su revelación concreta. Tal idea, patente siempre
con presencia inmediata o en expresión simbólica, no es
otra que la creencia en la capacidad del propio espíritu para
lograr la perfección de toda entidad humana: individuo o
sociedad (MFA, pp. 93-4).

Und das Leitmotiv?—Es klingt an in der ständig wieder-
holten Forderung nach Selbstbesinnung jedes einzelnen,
nach dem 'esfuerzo personal', und es tritt direkt auf in der
oben (s.S.196) von Ganivet selbst formulierten Fassung als
Abwandlung des Gedankens der 'autocreación', der, wirk-
sam in *Granada la bella*, im *Idearium español*, im Zyklus um
Pío Cid und besonders klar ausgeprägt in Titel und Inhalt
von dessen Abschluss, dem mystischen Drama *El escultor de
su alma*, uns nicht nur gestattet, Verbindungslinien zwischen
den einzelnen Schriften zu ziehen und Entwicklungen auf-
zuzeigen, sondern zugleich auch in sich Inhalt und Gehalt
von unsers Autors Leben und Werk fasst (Hans Jeschke, in
Revue Hispanique LXXII, 1928, 198).

El alma humana posee fuerza creadora, casi omnipotente, y
su misión es obrar sobre sí misma, para el propio perfec-
cionamiento. Labor íntima, de autocreación y moral robus-
tecimiento; que constituye el *leit-motiv* ganivetiano, y alcanza
su mayor desarrollo en *Los trabajos de Pío Cid* (QS, p. 180).

'Mantente de tal modo firme y erguido,' says Ganivet,
'que al menos se pueda decir siempre de ti que eres un
hombre' (152), and Láscaris Comneno, another of Ganivet's principal commentators, has given the following
explanation of this attitude:

La explicación de que Ganivet cifre la posture del hombre en
la *dignidad* se debe a considerar que ésta es la reacción
plausible en una vida que se vive a disgusto, contem-

plándola como un mal que, por ser inevitable, hay que soportar con entereza (in *Revista de la Universidad de Buenos Aires* XXII, 1952, 505).

Stoic morality, 'fundada legítimamente [. . .] sobre lo que subsiste aún en los periodos de mayor decadencia, el instinto de nuestra propia dignidad' (155), is Ganivet's answer to the misfortunes of existence and hence to the aboulic 'no querer' (and underlying 'no creer') that we examined in the previous section of this chapter. And as it is Ganivet's answer, so, in the *Idearium*, it becomes Spain's answer too, now under the name 'stoicism', now under the name 'spirit of independence'. The following passage, in which Ganivet urges the satisfaction of withdrawal and self-sufficiency on a personal plane, reflects exactly, I believe, his attitude to Spain:

Quizá el placer que se busca en vencer se encontraría retirándose. No es que yo me haga apóstol de la gandulería, pues se puede ser enérgico y activo en mil cosas que no se oponen a ningún hecho natural ni producen colisión de ningún género (II, 986).

The case, I suggest, is clear: the 'stoic' and 'independent' Spain of the *Idearium*, like the 'aboulic' Spain considered in my previous section, is the product of Ganivet's own mental and emotional state.

But here there is a problem, for in these last paragraphs we have seen that withdrawal and stoicism go hand in hand, that they are two aspects of the same response to life's misfortunes, whereas in Chapter III I showed that the two main 'fuerzas constituyentes' that Ganivet finds in the Spanish national character represent mutually opposing incentives to action. The difficulty, however, is not of my making, and before seeking to resolve it, I must

press again the essential similarity of stoicism and withdrawal (or 'spirit of independence'). I do so by quoting
Ganivet's summary of Senecan stoicism and inviting the
reader to consider it for a moment as an apostrophe to
Spain, with the replacement of the final words 'un hombre'
by the words 'una península'. The passage, I believe, will
then express exactly Ganivet's view of the territorial
spirit of independence (that is, his view of the need for
national withdrawal):

> No te dejes vencer por nada extraño a tu espíritu; piensa, en
> medio de los accidentes de la vida, que tienes dentro de ti
> una fuerza madre, algo fuerte e indestructible, como un
> eje diamantino, alrededor del cual giran los hechos mez-
> quinos que forman la trama del diario vivir; y sean cuales
> fueren los sucesos que sobre ti caigan, sean de los que
> llamamos prósperos, o de los que llamamos adversos, o de
> los que parecen envilecernos con su contacto, mantente de
> tal modo firme y erguido, que al menos se pueda decir
> siempre de ti que eres un hombre (152).

Withdrawal and stoicism, then, are closely related: one
withdraws in order to live 'lo más decente y filosóficamente posible'. On the other hand, the crusading fervour
that Ganivet claims to have evolved from stoicism represents a very different and even contradictory characteristic, and it is this that I earlier set up in conflict with the
territorial spirit of independence. But how can this conflict be explained in terms of Ganivet's own psychology?
How can crusading fervour coexist with his manifest
stoicism? We are touching here, I believe, on something
that is even more fundamental than the author's stoicism:
his desperate and ultimately futile search for an 'idea
directiva'.

His first doctorate thesis will serve again as our starting-

point. 'Los individuos y las colectividades,' he says, 'obran
guiados por una idea directiva' (II, 579-80). But in this
thesis, it will be remembered, Ganivet indicated only two
possible fields of faith, 'el espiritualismo y el materialismo',
and he took sides with neither. Nevertheless, Ganivet,
too, was fired by an ideal in the very writing of his thesis.
Philosophy, he says, which should offer guidance to men,
in fact ignores questions of present-day existence; 'la filosofía científica', the reserve of an intellectual minority, has
become divorced from 'la filosofía vulgar', 'la que es
patrimonio de todos los hombres, la que inspira la vida
de la sociedad y forma lo que generalmente se denomina
medio ambiente' (II, 579-81). Thereupon, he studied in
turn the present state of 'common philosophy' and of
'scientific philosophy', the reasons for their divorce, and
the means by which the existing situation could be im-
proved. It is a grandiose synthesis, belonging neither to
the realm of religious thought ('el espiritualismo') nor to
the realm of empirical thought ('el materialismo'). It
represents a third realm of faith that Ganivet exemplifies
but does not examine: faith in the idea and in one's ability
to reduce real-life complexities to the delightful simplicity
of an intellectual schema ('el idealismo'). Moreover, it is a
realm of faith to which Ganivet had apparently been
attracted at an early age. Here, as evidence, is the testi-
mony of his intimate friend, Nicolás María López:

> Ganivet no ha tenido propiamente juventud. Creo que
> desde que tiene uso de razón ha pasado los días pere-
> grineando por los libros y por mundos imaginarios (Pro-
> logue to *Cartas finlandesas*, Granada 1898, p. xlvii).

Perhaps Ganivet himself had this aspect of his childhood in mind when he recalled his 'seriedad ordinaria e

K

"impropia de mis años" " (II, 814), and the evidence that we
possess on his early years seems to point to a classic case
of the boy of modest circumstances who scholarships
himself to the top by dint of premature and excessive intellectualization and perhaps sacrifices too much in the
process, including his religious faith. At all events, Ganivet's delight in facile intellectualization is evident from his
first doctorate thesis and it is to a realm of ideas and ideals,
freed from the impurities of real-life contact, that he
aspires, with even greater ardour, when disillusion with
empirical study and the material world upon which it is
based is added to his lack of religious faith:

> Cuando la realidad es demasiado grosera, no hay más
> recurso que embrutecerse o idealizarse (19 May 1894; II,
> 972).

Ganivet chooses to idealize—on an ever-shrinking basis
of real-life contacts. 'Recogido dentro de mí mismo, por
falta de medios de comunicación, todas las fuerzas se
gastan en cavilar y barajar ideas y planes' (II, 907).

But idealization, for Ganivet, is not a process of mere
abstraction from material phenomena, however he may
champion the merits of abstraction against those of
analysis (above, pp. 130–1), and in this respect one can
compare the last inset quotation with the following:

> Después de concebir teóricamente una cosa como debe ser,
> y topar con ella tal y como es, no quedan más que dos cami-
> nos: el protestar enérgicamente y cubrirse la cabeza con el
> manto [. . .] o el de revolcarse en las tan acreditadas 'im-
> purezas de la realidad', y acochinarse, hablando en plata
> (25 May 1895; NML, p. 44).

When one is disgusted with reality, says Ganivet, there
are only two solutions: one can either allow oneself to be

dragged down by that reality ('embrutecerse' in the earlier quotation, 'acochinarse' in this one) or one can withdraw from it ('idealizarse' in the earlier quotation, 'cubrirse la cabeza con el manto' in this one). I find the latter equation extremely revealing and amply illustrated in Ganivet's writings.[1] Thus, of man's relationship with woman he writes:

> Delante de la hija de Eva que tira coces y huele, y no a ámbar, no queda más vía libre que la del hidalgo manchego ante la moza tobosina: tomar de ella la 'idea de sexo' nada más (el olor, como quien dice), y reconstruir sobre este pequeño cimiento un castillo imaginario que llegue hasta donde se pueda (19 May 1894; II, 971).

It is not enough, he continues, to search objectively for one's ideal, to try to find it by idealizing a real-life person; one must take from reality only the suggestion, the mere idea, and elaborate that idea within oneself. It is, of course, a purely defensive process, as can be seen from Ganivet's advice to Nicolás María López, involved in 'una aventura trágico-burguesa':

> En tales trances no queda otro recurso que idealizar, para que en el cuadro inmenso de lo ideal, las amarguras de carne y hueso resulten más pequeñas, y no den al traste con nosotros (25 May 1895; NML, p. 41).

Ganivet, then, does not merely abstract; he escapes into the inner world of his imaginings. It is 'perfectly stoic', he declares, to combine scorn of people as individuals with esteem for them as representatives of the human

---

[1] Besides complementing the earlier quotation, the later quotation also reminds us that, however much Ganivet's idealism may have been intensified by his disgust with reality, it was also the original cause of that disgust: 'Después de concebir teóricamente una cosa como debe ser, y topar con ella tal y como es . . .'

species such as one believes it to be represented *within oneself*:

> No deja de ser gracioso que un hombre a quien le revienten los ciudadanos aisladamente, sin exceptuar su mujer propia, se complazca en hacerles bien a bulto. Sin embargo, la idea es perfectamente estoica: menospreciar los individuos y exaltar la especie, la idea de Humanidad que cada cual cree está por él representada (17 November 1893; II, 925).

Even when Ganivet ventures outside this type of personal ideal realm and writes of those ideas which in a given age hover about all men and seem to be communicated through mysterious *ideaductos*, he is still not concerned with ideas in a purely conceptual sense: their content is both *ideal* and *espiritual*, and the author seems not to distinguish between the two terms (II, 938–9).

Ganivet, then, does not withdraw from reality merely in order to endure it better (stoicism); he withdraws also, still further, in order to re-create it within himself (idealism). 'Cuando uno no cree en nada y no desea nada, se queda uno en la gloria,' he says (NML, p. 58). External reality is crude, confused, disgusting, devoid of heroes and devoid of great ideals: 'el heroísmo anda de capa caída' (II, 820), 'ya no hay quien se meta a enderezar tuertos' (II, 929–30), 'ya nadie siente deseo de idealizar' (II, 972). We must therefore lift ourselves up from this material world and create our own personal ideal realm, 'degradarnos materialmente, pero regenerar nuestro espíritu, desembarazándolo de ligaduras que le entorpecen' (II, 972). 'Nada importa la pequeñez del medio,' Ganivet declares, 'si hay grandeza de ideal' (II, 951). Idealization, then, for Ganivet, is a means of escape from the horrors of reality into an inner world of self-indulgence in which *ideas*, *ideales* and *imaginaciones* are inextricably interwoven. And at this point one may recall the 'alegoría de la nave como símbolo de las cosas humanas' (199) to which I have attached such importance in an earlier chapter (above, pp. 119–21). The following passage was apparently inspired by a similar view from his house in Helsingfors and it illustrates the same point:

> Debajo de mi balcón está el embarcadero del barrio en que vivo, el Parque, y por él desfila toda la población para subir y bajar de los barcos que hacen el servicio de comunicación con el centro y otros barrios de la ciudad. Sin querer, en unos cuantos meses voy a saberme de memoria a toda esta patulea; pero de ahí no paso. Por los cuerpos adivino almas, y las almas me resultan cuerpos. Así como los rayos X sirven para penetrar más adentro, pero no para ver más, sino para no ver lo más tenue, así la observación concentrada de los objetos (de las personas quería decir) no nos descubre cada vez algo más espiritual, sino al contrario, cada vez algo más grosero [. . .]. El alma de la metafísica te he dicho mil veces, no es la observación: es la abstracción que obra sobre las formas reales exteriores e intenta reducirlas a la forma *una*. En cuanto cogemos el microscopio, la unidad se fue a freír morcilla (25 April 1896; in *Helios* II, 1903, 550–1).

There is no suggestion, either in this passage or in the corresponding passage from the *Idearium*, that abstraction gives a truer view of reality than close empirical study. Ganivet's insistence in his letter is on 'algo más espiritual' and reduction to 'la forma *una*', and his emphasis in the *Idearium* is on ideas as 'destello divino', born 'limpia[s] y sin mancha entre las espumas del pensamiento'. Ganivet's mental activity, I repeat, is not directed at dispassionate abstraction and systematization on a basis of external, real-life phenomena; it represents a flight from reality into a purely personal realm of ideals and imaginings. 'En las sombras que deja lo material,' he declares, 'nuestro espíritu dibuja todo un universo' (in *Helios* III, 1904, 166).

In short, stoicism, for Ganivet, is not enough. He is not content merely to defend himself against the misfortunes of human existence with a brave front of stoic virtues. He longs for something more positive, more idealistic, more grandiose. Stoicism, one feels, despite its manifest importance in Ganivet's mental constitution—and thence also in *Idearium español*—is there only as a form of Cartesian 'provisional morality' whilst the author elaborates his own intensely personal 'universo'. Reality and the ideal, necessity and desire, fatalism and the will, withdrawal and expansion, and, embracing all these dualities, stoicism and fervour—*Idearium español*, like its author, moves incessantly between these extremes. In Chapter III we examined the oscillations as they reveal themselves in the *Idearium*, and now, in these last pages, we have discovered them also in the author's spiritual biography.[1] The simi-

---

[1] Similarly, against Ganivet's much proclaimed stoic reserve ('austero y reservado', NML, p. 12) and his 'espíritu de abnegación y de amor' (NML, in MP, 1920, p. 167) is to be set his 'vehemencia que no puede ser igualada por nadie' (Miguel Utrillo, in *La Estafeta Literaria*, 30 March 1944). Perhaps the former was Ganivet's attitude to friends who accepted his authority, and the latter his attitude to passing acquaintances who presumed to question it. At all events, Utrillo's quotation of his father's eye-witness account of Ganivet in Catalonia is a valuable antidote to the view of the man that is usually expressed:

El pobre Ganivet era un anormal; discutía con una vehemencia que no puede ser igualada por nadie: cuando defendía un criterio lo sostenía ferozmente. Se ponía frenético, pálido, desencajado, babeaba y cuando la cosa se ponía tan grave que debía terminarse lógicamente por vías de hecho, se levantaba del asiento y se marchaba. Y así casi todos los días.

Cualquier tema político o artístico era discutido así. Sobre todo los asuntos que afectaban a la soberanía de la autoridad política, le descomponían. Había en él un africano lleno de grandes pasiones y odios (loc. cit.).

larities, I suggest, are not fortuitous. As with aboulia and as with withdrawal, so also with stoicism and fervour Ganivet projects on to Spain what he has found in his own self-probing. The following passage, written in October 1893, illustrates admirably the conflict that two and a half years later he was to seek to rationalize in *Idearium español*:

Y donde se demuestra con más claridad nuestra positiva decadencia es comparando el papel que nosotros desempeñamos hoy. Nosotros, los que más debíamos pensar en las cosas africanas, que quizá con el tiempo podrían ser nuestras propias cosas, no sabemos hoy de la misa la media de lo que ocurre, mientras no hay nación de Europa que no meta baza en estos asuntos y no procure sacar astilla por lo que pudiere tronar. De aquí que no pudiendo intervenir, como no podemos materialmente, se me haya ocurrido a mí intervenir con la pluma [. . .].

[. . .] Tengo por seguro que 'comulgarás' con *El Imparcial* y que arderás en entusiasmo patriótico, pues otra cosa no se puede esperar de tan legítimo español como tú. Si quieres que te diga la verdad, esas salidas de tono que ahí producen efecto muy deplorable, en el extranjero lo causan bueno, y contribuyen a que se consoliden nuestros derechos a intervenir en Marruecos el día que llegue la hora de la disolución. La opinión se va formando poco a poco, y tanto se repite una idea, que al fin llega a parecer natural hasta a aquellos que la creyeron al principio irrealizable. Por estas veinticuatro horas, la opinión exterior, esa que se siente, aunque no se vea en letras de molde, es que España está llamada a intervenir más tarde, no siendo hoy posible porque no estamos preparados ni tenemos prestigio para que las demás naciones nos hagan el caso debido.

Si España tuviera fuerzas para salir de la tregua actual, que la obliga a restaurarse por los cuatro costados antes de decir esta boca es mía, y pudiera 'inclinarse' a cualquier grupo de los que están en Europa arma al brazo, nuestra intervención en Marruecos era cosa de éxito seguro. Pero yo creo que ni en cincuenta años nos conviene todavía cargarnos con ese fardo tan pesado y con las obligaciones que traería consigo. Y claro está que no siendo posible ir al fin, será casi inútil todo lo que se haga. Será una demostración nueva de nuestra intención, pero resultado práctico ninguno. Y a todo esto falta un detalle importante, y es que entre tanto como se habla y se chilla no suena ninguna *voz de hombre*, del hombre que haya de hacer *eso* (21 October 1893; II, 912–14).

The oscillations are obvious: on the one hand, the realistic acceptance of Spain's limitations; on the other, the ill-disguised hope that Spain will one day be able to intervene in Africa and the consoling anticipation of 'éxito seguro'. And hovering over it all, the threat of the dictatorial '*voz de hombre*, del hombre que haya de hacer *eso*'. But, for the moment, Ganivet can see no chance of real-life success. 'De aquí que no pudiendo intervenir, como no podemos materialmente, se me haya ocurrido a mí intervenir con la pluma'. The outcome was *La conquista del reino de Maya*, in which a fictional hero undertook the conquests that the author and his country could only dream of.[1]

It would seem from the evidence so far presented that, despite the emphasis on withdrawal and stoicism in the *Idearium*, Ganivet does not really want these, either for his country or for himself. And here one may recall an earlier quotation:

---

[1] There is no place here, of course, to examine the irony of the novel. In the *Conquista* as in the *Idearium* Ganivet oscillates between realistic containment and idealistic fervour. In the *Idearium*, however, the basis is that of containment, with intoxicated flights towards the ideal; in the *Conquista*, on the other hand, the basis is that of the ideal, with ironic falls towards disillusioning reality.

Quizá el placer que se busca en vencer se encontraría
retirándose. No es que yo me haga apóstol de la gandulería,
pues se puede ser enérgico y activo en mil cosas que no se
oponen a ningún hecho natural ni producen colisión de
ningún género (II, 986).

Ganivet is referring here to his personal situation but the
words recall forcibly those 'fantasies of imperialism and
conquest' on which, in part at least, he turns his back in
the *Idearium* (above, p. 88):

¿Puede darse nada más bello que civilizar salvajes, que
conquistar nuevos pueblos a nuestra religión, a nuestras
leyes y a nuestro idioma? (260)

Moreover, it is worth noting the following confession
from his exchange with Unamuno on the future of Spain:

Si España tuviera fuerzas para trabajar en Africa, yo, que
soy un quídam, me comprometería a inventar media docena
de teorías nuevas para que nos quedáramos legalmente con
cuanto se nos antojara (II, 1078).

In view of such statements—and they are not alone—it
is surely not unfair to see in Ganivet's insistence on
withdrawal from 'el placer que se busca en vencer' a
considerable element of sour grapes. Indeed, Laín Entralgo has pointed to evidence of this attitude in a more
limited field,[1] Ganivet's own much quoted derision of the
function of a Professor of Greek after he himself had
failed to be appointed to a Chair of Greek is a clear example from his own biography,[2] and Bertrand Russell has

[1] He notes a conflict between 'el hombre Ganivet' who esteemed and
desired 'la técnica', and 'el español Ganivet' who has a fox-and-the-
grapes attitude to it ('como la vulpeja ante el racimo') (In *Ensayos y
Estudios*, II, 1940, 70).
[2] Claro está que el barcelonés, persona respetabilísima por otra parte,
fue quien se llevó la cátedra. Y Ganivet decía:—La verdad es que no

drawn attention to 'an element of sour grapes' in stoicism in general.[1]

It is, of course, a form of self-defence, a means of stopping up the abyss between longing and attainment. 'Nada hay más doloroso,' Ganivet observes, 'que ambicionar grandezas que están fuera de nuestra acción' (NML, p. 57). And as Russell points out, the stoic doctrine is useful in a bad world, even if it is not quite true or even sincere. And this, surely, was its appeal to Ganivet. For to him, certainly, the world seemed especially bad. But Ganivet does not stop at stoicism; his ultimate aim is that inner, personal 'universo' of his own imaginings, and its therapeutic function is obvious. 'Desde que no creemos en nada,' says Ganivet, 'tenemos necesidad de inventar todas las mañanas unos cuantos dogmas que nos permitan pasar el día como seres racionales' (II, 868). And in so far as Ganivet's 'dogmas' and idealizings and imaginings serve purely personal therapeutic ends, 'para vivir lo más decente y filosóficamente posible' (II, 926) amidst a world that he despises, 'para disfrazar las miserias de la vida e impedir que se acerque la idea del suicidio' (II, 1016–17),

---

sabe el favor que me ha hecho, porque ¿cómo será posible amar a Homero teniendo que analizarle y traducirle a diario en clase? Tanto valdría estar casado con la Venus de Milo. —Y luego anadía—: ¿Qué cara pondría una mujer un poco lista y espiritual que después de haberse enamorado románticamente de un hombre, y en un momento de expansión y deliquio llegase a averiguar que el objeto de sus ansias era un señor profesor de lengua griega? (F. Navarro Ledesma, Prologue to *Epistolario*, 1904, p. 25).

[1] There is, in fact, an element of sour grapes in Stoicism. We can't be happy, but we can be good; let us therefore pretend that, so long as we are good, it doesn't matter being unhappy. This doctrine is heroic, and, in a bad world, useful; but it is neither quite true nor, in a fundamental sense, quite sincere (*A History of Western Philosophy*, London 1946, pp. 291–2).

The qualities with which Ganivet is concerned are different, but Russell's criticism is clearly relevant.

we need take no exception to them. It is for every human
being to choose the opium best suited to himself. Nor do
I presume to question Ganivet's right to live in a realm of
ideas that reflects no reality but that of his own mind.
However, one must be concerned when Ganivet attempts
to project his ideas outwards on to others. It is a real
danger in a theorist who is convinced that men in general
are fools in need of despotic rule, and who believes that
a genius is required to give them the guidance of an ideal:

> Se necesita ser un *genio* para sacar a una multitud de su
> bajeza y elevarla a la contemplación ideal simultánea [. . .];
> la Humanidad entera no es nada mientras no hay un ojo que
> la vea y un cerebro que la traduzca en ideas, que son las
> formas de representación subjetiva (27 November 1893; II,
> 927).

Doubtless Ganivet already felt himself tempted by the
role.[1] Knowledge and feeling together, he says, give will
and creative force (II, 831), and alongside the Ganivet
abúlico there is also, at moments, the Ganivet who believes
that the will is his strong point (II, 883). And is he not an
admirer of Napoleon, 'que no comprendía el modo de
seguir la ruta indicada, sino el de echar por los cerros de
Ubeda y convertir una obra colectiva en personalísima'
(II, 992)? But Taine, whose view Ganivet is here dis-
cussing, extols Napoleon for his inexhaustible attention
to real-life phenomena.[2] How different from his Spanish

---

[1] We all know, says Juan del Rosal, 'el apasionado entusiasmo de
Angel por las tareas docentes' (*Del pensar y vivir*, Madrid 1943, p. 26). And
recall Ganivet's *alter ego*, Pío Cid:
> A ratos pienso que quien está a mi cabecera no es una pobre sirvienta,
> sino España, toda España, que viene a aprender a leer, escribir y
> pensar, y con esta idea se me va el santo al cielo, y me explayo como
> si estuviera en una llanura sin horizontes (II, 43).

[2] H. Taine, *Les Origines de la France contemporaine: Le régime moderne*,
I, Paris 1891, pp. 3–116, especially pp. 23–34.

admirer who makes a merit of ignoring all but the 'idea' of reality, which he then uses as the mere starting-point for his self-confessed personal imaginings! 'No es que las ideas se van a perder,' he declares; 'es que se va a escapar de nuestro dominio la inteligencia' (II, 812). Exactly, and this, in essence, is my criticism of *Idearium español*, for the *Idearium*, I suggest, is not a serious intellectual work; it is a work of intoxicated, therapeutic intellectualization.

CONCLUSION

In this chapter I have tried to show that both in his diagnosis of aboulia and in the 'fuerzas constituyentes' upon which he bases his oscillating prescription for national cure Ganivet projects on to Spain the basic aspects of his own spiritual crisis. I have confined myself to what I find to be fundamental in the *Idearium* and have thus omitted mention of several more detailed and more obvious cases of the author's self-projection; his projection on to Spain and its alleged 'espíritu guerrero' of his own impatience with organization and administrative restraints;[1] his presentation of his countrymen's 'espíritu jurídico' in terms that clearly reflect his own distaste for the legal profes-

---

[1] odio con toda mi alma nuestra organización y todas sus infinitas farsas, y veré con entusiasmo todos los trabajos de destrucción, aunque sea yo el primero que perezca (II, 1010).

Todo idealista sincero tiene que ir a parar a la anarquía, pues no encontrará medios de acomodarse a transacciones deshonestas. Cuando yo era bibliotecario deseaba que suprimiesen todas las bibliotecas, y ahora desearía que quitasen de un medio todos los consulados (NML, p. 44).

Incidentally, I find in the latter passage a clear answer to the frequently expressed view that Ganivet 'hubiera podido desahogadamente gobernar con el mismo acierto e idéntica seguridad con que escribía' (C. Román, in *El País*, 30 November 1903).

sion;[1] his description of the typical Spanish artist with
words that, however badly they suit Velázquez, apply admirably to Ganivet himself.[2] Such cases, I repeat, are
obvious and they need concern us no further. My view
of the *Idearium* as a spiritual autobiography must stand or
fall on the case that I have made for aboulia and for
Spain's various alleged 'fuerzas constituyentes'. And in
all these things, I find, Ganivet's interpretation of Spain
stems clearly from his own self-probing.

But underlying the *Idearium* there is perhaps an even
more intimate and more important element of spiritual
autobiography, for the very writing of the work, I suggest,
may itself have been a form of personal therapeutic, a
means for Ganivet to justify his own crisis by finding it
also in his country, and, at the same time, an opportunity
for him to substitute, in one area of experience, the
delight of 'ideas limpias y sin mancha' for the complexity
and confusion of 'la impureza inseparable de lo material'.
And here, of course, would be the special appeal to him of
determinism. After all, what greater delight, for a fatalist
who is also an idealist, than a system that views phenomena in a vast network of inevitability and, in synthesis,
adapts them to the pure lines of an intellectual schema?
'Il n'y a rien de réel dans la nature,' wrote Taine, 'sauf des

---

[1] The following extract from a recent study brings together relevant
evidence:

    [Ganivet] había comprobado que él, que había 'estudiado leyes' no
podría nunca 'ver el mecanismo judicial por su lado noble y serio' y
tomó su decisión, luego de una ligera pasantía: 'Antes pediré limosna
que ejercer la abogacía ni nada que roce con ella'. Su sentido estricto
del ideal jurídico le llevó incluso a alejarse de la Academia de Juris-
prudencia, que tan grata le era, 'por incompatibilidad de humores con
la parva de ministros en agraz que por allí pululaban' (Luis Aguirre
Prado, *Ganivet*, Madrid 1965, p. 9).

[2] es preferible una majadería propia que una genialidad ajena (NML,
p. 56).

trames d'évènements liés entre eux et à d'autres, et il n'y a
rien de plus en nous-mêmes ni en autre chose.'[1] Whatever
facts Taine may in practice have sought to synthesize in
his studies, the theory allows for a wide range of individual interpretation, and Ganivet chose the interpretation most suited to himself with his growing 'repulsión
espiritual contra la realidad' (II, 811): facts are unworthy;
'lo que realmente vive son las ideas' (221).

I conclude with an extract from a letter written in 1896
to Nicolás María López. It is relevant to many of the
points discussed in this chapter, and it tells us much of
Ganivet's state of mind during the writing of *Idearium
español*:

> He querido ser siempre amo de mí mismo; tener siempre la
> cabeza en su sitio, sin hacer nada de que ella no tuviere cono-
> cimiento; y decía yo que el día que mi cabeza se cansara de
> dirigir el cotarro, el día que mi voluntad se blandeara, sería
> el desquiciamiento de todos los órganos de mi infeliz per-
> sonalidad; y sin embargo, yo tocaba el violón, puesto que
> me ha ocurrido lo contrario. Hace algunos años que me
> abandoné al fatalismo, y que llegué a no tener *propósitos*, ni a
> pensar reflexivamente en lo que hacía; hoy me encuentro en
> un estado de postración espiritual que a ti mismo te daría
> lástima, y ahora es cuando trabajo más, sin saber cómo, sin
> hacerme cargo, ni tener idea de lo que me sale; no sé si es
> bueno o malo; pero sospecho que es mejor de lo que antes
> hacía, y me dejaba la impresión de algo discreto. Es decir,
> que ahora podré cometer majaderías estupendas, sin estar en
> mi mano enmendarlas ni conocerlas; pero quizás me salga
> algo que las compense. Estoy componiendo un libro pequeño
> (pues no me gustan los grandes), una ideología que desde
> luego te aseguro es mejor que lo que hace . . . (29 August
> 1896; NML, p. 69).

[1] H. Taine, *De l'Intelligence*, 3rd ed., vol. II, Paris 1878, p. 5.

The 'pequeño libro' is the *Idearium* itself; the 'majaderías estupendas' are the ideas expressed in it. As manifestations of a spiritual crisis and an attempt at personal therapeutics, they are fascinating, 'estupendas'; as a probing of the problem of Spain they are, as Ganivet himself suggests, 'majaderías'.

VI

IDEARIUM ESPAÑOL AS LITERATURE

Ganivet's *Idearium*, we have seen, has a clearer and more systematic progression than has generally been acknowledged. In the first part of his book (A), the author affirms the existence of two main 'fuerzas constituyentes' of the Spanish soul—stoicism evolving to fervour, and the spirit of independence—and thereafter seeks to confirm this by reference to three spheres of national activity: military, legal and artistic. In the second part (B), he examines Spanish history in the light of these 'fuerzas constituyentes', finds that the country has weakened itself by acting against its basic spirit of independence, and urges the concentration of energies within the country as a necessary preliminary to spiritual leadership of the Hispanic world. Finally, in his third section (C), Ganivet finds that the Spanish nation is suffering from mental illness because of its inability to see where its true path lies, urges again the need for spiritual regeneration on the basis of essential and inescapable traditions, and again emphasizes Spain's qualifications for ideal leadership.

It is a manifestly determinist approach to Spanish civilization, and there is evident influence of nineteenth-century thought about biological evolution: in the emphasis on civilization as an organism of interdependent parts, in the search for the all-pervading 'fuerzas céntricas' (the 'hidden bonds of connection') that different periods of the same civilization have in common, in the acceptance of self-preservation as a fundamental general principle that manifests itself differently in different physical environments and, finally, in the notion that healthy development presupposes adaptation to physical environment. Expressions of the type 'la ley natural', 'la fuerza natural', 'nuestra natural evolución' and 'el principio general [. . .] la conservación' are both characteristic and significant (above, pp. 98–9).

But Ganivet's immediate influence, I have suggested, was the French determinist historian and philosopher Hippolyte Taine, whose works Ganivet was reading 'de cabo a rabo' during his stay in Antwerp (II, 829) and who likewise rejoiced in the thought that 'aujourd'hui l'histoire comme la zoologie a trouvé son anatomie' (*HLA*, I, xii) and likewise sought to apply concepts and terminology derived from the natural sciences to his probings of national psychology. Like Ganivet, so also Taine before him aimed to look beneath the external manifestations of a given civilization and to arrive at the fundamental, all-pervading 'faculté maîtresse', 'quelque disposition primitive, [. . .] quelque trait propre à toutes les sensations, à toutes les conceptions d'un siècle ou d'une race, [. . .] quelque particularité inséparable de toutes les démarches de son esprit et de son cœur' (*HLA*, I, xvii), and thereafter to uphold this as the ideal centre to which the various external manifestations of the civilization could be shown to be related. Of course, there are also differences between the two writers, and in particular, Ganivet's fusion of race and environment into a single immutable influence and his scant attention to Taine's significant 'moment' makes his study notably more rigid and less subtle than those of the French writer. But basically both writers are similar in their approach, and their work suffers from a similar basic defect: an exaggerated emphasis on a simple, central, all-pervading 'idea', with consequent attempts to justify that 'idea' by possibly unjustified selection from the boundless complexity of the civilization presented. The use of literature as mere document and the elastic use of the words *idea* and *ideal* are two consequences of this approach that have been noted in the *Idearium* (above, pp. 113–21).

Fortified by his determinist faith and his 'ideal' view of Spanish civilization, Ganivet sets out to convince his reader. The following paragraph, in which he makes his case for stoicism, will serve as an illustration:

Sin necesidad de buscar relaciones subterráneas entre la doctrina de Séneca y la moral del cristianismo, se puede establecer entre ellas una relación patente e innegable, puesto que ambas son como el término de una evolución y el comienzo de otra evolución en sentido contrario, ambas se encuentran y se cruzan, como viajeros que vienen en opuestas direcciones y han de continuar caminando cada uno de ellos por el camino que el otro recorrió ya. El término de una evolución filosófica racional, como la grecorromana, es, cuando están todas las soluciones agotadas: la empírica y la constructiva, la materialista y la idealista, la ecléctica y la sincrética; la solución negativa o escéptica; y entonces surge la moral estoica, moral sin base, fundada solo en la virtud o en la dignidad; pero esa solución es transitoria, porque bien pronto el hombre, menospreciando las fuerzas de su razón que no le conducen a nada positivo, cierra los ojos y acepta una creencia. El término de una evolución teológica, como la del pueblo hebreo, tiene que ser también, cuando ya están agotadas todas las soluciones históricas, esto es, todos los modos de acción, una solución negativa, anarquista, diríamos hoy: tal era la que anunciaban los profetas; y entonces debe surgir una moral que, como la cristiana, condene la acción y vea en ella la causa de los sufrimientos humanos y reconstruya la sociedad sobre la quietud, el desprendimiento y el amor; pero esa moral es transitoria, porque bien pronto el hombre, desengañado de la fe que le conduce a producir actos negativos, se acoge a la razón; y comienza una segunda evolución que ya no se muestra en actos, sino en ideologías (154).

With what confidence Ganivet guides his reader to an understanding of this 'relación patente e innegable' between Seneca's doctrines and Christian morality! With what assurance he traces the essential line of Graeco-Roman philosophy and the essential line of Hebrew religion, and how superficially satisfying the basic parallel that he establishes between the two of them! Facts would confuse the issue. Ganivet's concern is not with men but with man (*el hombre*), not with philosophies and theologies but with philosophy and theology. And he is concerned with these things as elements in an evolving system of causal relationships. Since Ganivet claims to understand that system with a certainty that allows prediction, he must present each successive stage as inevitable. The expressions *han de continuar*, *tiene que ser* and *debe surgir* are characteristic manifestations of his proclaimed understanding. Here are a few similar examples from the immediately following five pages:[1]

la moral cristiana, aunque *lógicamente* nacida de la religión judaica, . . . (154-5)

Y así *por este encadenamiento natural*, el cristianismo . . . (155)

Lo noble, lo justo, lo humanitario, sostenido y amparado solo por la razón, . . . *no puede ni podrá jamás* vencer las pasiones bajas . . .; para encadenar la fuerza irresponsable de los grandes . . ., *hay que* confundirlos a todos . . . (155)

[1] In all cases the italics are mine.

Los que se maravillan de la rápida y al parecer inexplicable propagación del cristianismo, *debían considerar* cómo destruida la religión pagana por la filosofía, y la filosofía por los filósofos, *no quedaba más salida que* . . .; y los que se espantan ante el sangriento holocausto de los mártires innumerables, *debían pensar* que . . . (155-6)

Sin su sacrificio, Jesús hubiera sido un moralista más, y *sin el sacrificio de los mártires,* el cristianismo hubiera sido una moral más . . . (156)

Todas las religiones y en general todas las ideas se han propagado y propagan y propagarán en igual forma (156)

porque *¿qué admiración puede causar* que . . .? (156)

en España, donde era el asiento del estoicismo más *lógico,* . . . (157)

ese esfuerzo no fue en un principio, como *debió ser,* un esfuerzo creador (157)

los filósofos cristianos . . . *eligieron como tontos* (157)

Esa evolución, sin embargo, no fue igual *ni pudo serlo* en las diversas provincias del Imperio romano, . . . *ni* esa unidad *pudo mantenerse* (157)

Los historiadores aficionados a las antítesis y a los contrastes *pretenden convencernos* de que . . . *La verdad es,* al contrario, que . . . (158)

Si los bárbaros hubieran podido moverse con libertad, *hubieran dislocado* en breve el cristianismo (158)

La ruina del poder godo *tiene su explicación* en ese artificio gubernativo (159)

el periodo visigótico, que *para los que se fijan solo en aparien- cias* es trascendental y decisivo en la formación de nuestro espíritu religioso, es, a mi juicio, importante solo de una manera externa (159)

They are all characteristic expressions, and examples would simply be multiplied by reference to other pages of the book. Among those listed above some insist on the logic and naturalness and even the necessity of the developments described;[1] others show the author seeking to integrate his determinist view of Spanish civilization into a wider pattern of causality;[2] in yet others he criticizes historians—and even historical personages—for not recognizing and accepting the underlying forces of civilization that he himself feels able to affirm with such confidence;[3] finally—still within these few pages that in this

[1] *lógicamente*; *por este encadenamiento natural*; *hay que*; *no quedaba más salida que*; *¿qué admiración puede causar?*; *lógico*; *ni pudo serlo ... ni pudo mantenerse*; *tiene su explicación*. Note also, in the same pages: *y así*; *por esto*; *por esta razón*; *de suerte que*; *de tal suerte que*; *de donde*; *puesto que*; *porque*. And one can consider here Professor Geyl's criticism of another, better documented but similarly over-confident, approach to 'the unruly and indomitable complexity of historical reality':
'It will be seen.' This [. . .] is, as usual, a gratuitous assertion that this description must carry conviction to the mind of the average unbiased reader, for, also as usual, the facts have been marshalled in accordance with the writer's pre-conceived conclusion. 'Thanks only', 'patently', it all comes out of the bag of tricks, not of the scholar, but of the orator out to persuade or, if need be, to bluff (*Debates with Historians*, London 1955, p. 161).
[2] *no puede ... ni podrá jamás*; *todas las religiones y en general todas las ideas se han propagado y propagan y propagarán en igual forma*. Notice also, in the same pages: *como*; *así como ... así también*; *tan ... como*. Here, too, Professor Geyl's sobering insistence on 'the infinite complexity and intangibility of the historical process' is clearly relevant (op. cit., p. 171 and elsewhere).
[3] *debían considerar. . . debían pensar*; *como debió ser*; *eligieron como tontos*; *pretenden convencernos*; *los que se fijan solo en apariencias*. Notice also, in the same pages, *al parecer* and *aparentemente* to indicate the appearances that have misled others but behind which, *en secreto*, operate the important forces that Ganivet himself has found. On this 'satanic enemy of true history, the mania for making judgments' (Bloch, *The Historian's Craft*, p. 31), recall Croce:
Those who on the plea of narrating history bustle about as judges, condemning here and giving absolution there, because they think this is the office of history, taking history's metaphorical tribunal in a material sense, are generally recognized as devoid of historical sense (*History as the Story of Liberty*, p. 47).

respect are characteristic of the whole book—some of the lines quoted illustrate Ganivet's manifest delight in hypothesizing, on the basis of his determinist system, about what would have happened if particular circumstances had been different.[1] It is the point at which intellectualization loses itself in dreams. *La conquista del reino de Maya* is an extended hypothesis of just this kind.

Underlying all the examples quoted above is Ganivet's apparently unquestioning confidence in the validity of his simple, determinist, 'ideal' view of civilizations in general and of Spanish civilization in particular. But it is not sufficient for an author to have confidence in his own particular view of a given reality; he must seek to communicate that confidence to his readers. At one extreme, a Menéndez Pidal will do this by careful logical argument on the basis of an impressive store of facts; at the other, an Azorín will seek to captivate his reader and make him suspend his critical disbelief by the evocative, emotive, magical use of language. What is Ganivet's method? After all, the success of the work during the seventy years since it first appeared is undeniable. By what means, then, has the author convinced his readers? This is the question with which we are here principally concerned. The preceding pages offer an initial pointer: the work is appealing, first, in its apparent simplicity, in the way in which Ganivet integrates his material into an apparently comprehensive and all-explaining intellectual schema and, secondly, in the authority that he appears to give to this schema by his frequent use of terminology and concepts derived from the natural sciences. Moreover, this second

[1] *Sin su sacrificio, Jesús hubiera sido . . . y sin el sacrificio de los mártires . . . Si los bárbaros hubieran . . .* Recall E. H. Carr on 'what I may call the "might-have-been" school of thought—or rather of emotion' (*What is History?*, pp. 90–3).

characteristic would be especially appealing during the early decades of the book's fame, when many students of civilization, including Unamuno, Azorín and Ortega y Gasset in Spain, were themselves much influenced by the methods of the natural sciences. But because of Ganivet's fusion of race and environment into a single immutable influence, and because of his general neglect of Taine's significant 'moment', the basic schema proposed in the *Idearium*, I have claimed, is unusually narrow and rigid —always excepting, of course, the false flexibility that is afforded to the work by the *deus ex machina* of stoicism evolving to crusading fervour. Consequently, I ask again: By what means has the author convinced his reader? And the question can now be reduced to another: How does Ganivet help us to bridge the chasm between his essentially naïve and over-simplified basic schema and the real-life complexity that he pretends to explain? It is with this question that I am now concerned.

An example of one of his most effective means of convincing his reader has just been referred to and was examined at length in Chapter III: by proposing a duality of independence and crusading fervour Ganivet allows himself freedom to explain, with apparent conviction, the most diverse tendencies in Spain's foreign policy and at the same time allows each reader the satisfaction of justifying his own preconceptions about Spain's future by reference to whichever of the proposed poles he finds more appropriate. And though this is the most important example of such a duality in *Idearium español*, it is not the only one. Ganivet, with his delight in hypothesis, appears to rejoice in the freedom of movement that such dualities permit. Thus, when he affirms that the 'fundamento invariable' of Europe's juridical evolution is 'la idea romana,

la fuerza, en pugna con la idea cristiana, el amor' (201–2),
the range of end-products that his duality could explain is
clearly limitless: from the absolute predominance of the
Roman 'idea' in one country, to the absolute predominance of the Christian 'idea' in another. As with the
duality of independence and fervour, the reader can take
his stand where he wishes. Similarly, in another passage
Ganivet affirms:

> o los hombres tienden por naturaleza a construir un solo
> organismo homogéneo, o tienden a acentuar las diferencias
> que existen entre sus diversas agrupaciones (167–8).

Again the range of possibilities seems limitless. But Ganivet sees a loophole in this duality and immediately seeks
to block it by dismissing with insults the possible 'insigne
mentecato' who might suggest [as anthropologists now
suggest] that man does not by nature tend in either direction. I offer two further examples without comment. In
both of them, I believe, the duality of extremes is obvious:

> En el enfermo de abulia las ideas carecen de esta funda-
> mental condición: la sociabilidad, por lo cual sus esfuerzos
> intelectuales carecen de eficacia. En unos casos la idea fija,
> que es la que influye más enérgicamente sobre la voluntad,
> produce la determinación arrebatada, violenta, que alguien
> confunde con la del alienado; en otros, la idea abstracta o la
> idea ya vieja, reproducida por la memoria, engendran el
> deseo débil, impotente, irrealizable (292).

> Unas veces el móvil será la tradición, que jamás puede
> producir, aunque otra cosa se crea, un impulso enérgico,
> porque en la vida intelectual lo pasado, así como es centro
> poderoso de resistencia, es principio débil de actividad;
> otras veces se obedecerá a una fuerza extraña, pues las
> sociedades débiles, como los artistas de pobre ingenio,
> suplen con las imitaciones la falta de propia inspiración (293).

Ganivet, then, relaxes the basic rigidity of his system by proposing dualities that explain the most varied phenomena. He relaxes it also by his rather uncritical 'agility' in the use of words and concepts. Several examples have been noted in earlier chapters: the oscillating role that he ascribes to reason in his treatment of stoicism (above, pp. 73–4), his unwary use of the terms *agresión, resistencia* and *independencia* (above, pp. 75–7), the possibility or impossibility of success by a leader whose 'idea' is 'ajena al pensamiento y al sentimiento generales' (above, pp. 77–8) . . .[1] Here a single further example will suffice. It pertains to Ganivet's elastic use of the word 'ideal' to conceal his lack of clear thought about Spain's basic 'fuerzas constituyentes':

> más importante que la tendencia ideal de un arte es la concepción y ejecución de la obra, o sea, *la obra en sí* [. . .]. Mientras el fondo del arte procede de la constitución ideal de la raza, la técnica arranca del espíritu territorial (212).

The lines are from Ganivet's third illustration of Spain's alleged 'fuerzas constituyentes' in action: his section on Spanish art. The 'tendencia ideal' of art, he says, refers to its content and is the outcome of the nation's 'constitución ideal', at the basis of which he earlier found stoicism (151) but now finds an alleged development from

[1] Cf. Nicolás María López, who finds 'algunas palabras tomadas en sentido equívoco' and alleges misuse of the word 'sensualidad' (Prologue to *Cartas finlandesas*, 1898, pp. xxii–xxiii); Melchor Fernández Almagro, who notes 'ese impreciso uso del vocablo *misticismo*, que [. . .] confunde con *ascetismo*' (MFA, p. 115); Manuel Azaña, who criticizes Ganivet for his uncritical use of the words *pueblo, nación* and *raza*, and for his play on the word *capitán* ['Para presentar ante Europa una figura militar de primer orden,' says Ganivet, 'tenemos que acudir a un capitán nada más, al Gran Capitán, etc. (188)] (*Plumas y palabras*, Madrid 1930, pp. 28, 93). In this last respect one might recall that the Duke of Marlborough was known to his men as 'Corporal John'. But perhaps corporals are aggressive where captains are merely independent.

stoicism: the fervour of mysticism ('el fondo del arte es
la religión en su sentido más elevado, el misticismo', 212).
On the other hand, says Ganivet, the technique, 'la concepción y ejecución de la obra, o sea, *la obra en sí*', stems
from the territorial spirit of independence. But as stoicism
—or fervour—is at the basis of Spain's 'constitución
ideal' (151), so also the spirit of independence is at the
basis of Spain's 'evolución ideal' (175). Consequently, we
reveal the laxity of Ganivet's terminology—but do no in-
justice to his thought—by re-writing the second sentence
of the last inset quotation as follows: 'mientras el fondo
del arte procede de la constitución ideal de la raza, la
técnica arranca de [su evolución ideal]'. Ganivet's in-
toxication with ideals has clearly led him to use the word
ideal as a mere blanket term to conceal the inadequacies of
his thought and to mesmerize the unwary reader.

Nor is it only words and concepts that mislead in this
way. Ganivet's arguments, too, are at times given an
appearance of logic that they do not merit, as, for example, when he seeks to justify his claim that stoicism is a
basic, distinguishing characteristic of Spain's 'constitución ideal' by upholding it as common to the Roman
Empire at a particular moment in time. Images, too,
frequently mislead in a similar way, and here one recalls
especially the abundance of 'natural' imagery that is so
characteristic of Ganivet's age: the notion of the marked
out 'path of history' ('el cauce que le estaba marcado',
219); the view of colonies as 'hijos de la carne' (151), as
'nuestra numerosa familia' (244), as 'hermanos efectivos'
(252); the presentation of the 'fuerzas constituyentes del
alma de un país' in terms of anatomy and physiology (209).
Ganivet's contrast between the development of Latin
American nations and that of the United States (244–56)

exemplifies admirably the misleading type of imagery to which I refer and to which modern historians have taken exception.[1] At one point it seems that Ganivet himself glimpses the danger of imagery when he writes: 'El poder de la metáfora en el mundo es inmenso y a veces nocivo' (163). But thereupon—unwittingly, one assumes—he proceeds to offer the reader an example from his own store, for having begged the question about the existence of an 'ideal centre', he continues:

> No hay, pues, medio de escape: podemos alejarnos cuanto queramos del centro ideal que nos rige; podemos describir órbitas inmensas; pero siempre tendremos que girar alrededor del eterno centro (165).

Such examples could be listed at length, for if there is one thing that Ganivet does illustrate adequately in his *Idearium* it is the misleading nature of imagery. Here, however, a single further example must suffice. It is contained in the first paragraph of the book, is fundamental to Ganivet's view of Spain, and its scant justification was first pointed out by Unamuno in 1898 (*OC* IV, 1958, 966–7). Briefly, Ganivet confuses the dogma of the Immaculate

---

[1] Here a single sentence must serve to recall Ganivet's treatment:
Las naciones hispanoamericanas no han pasado de la infancia, en tanto que los Estados Unidos han comenzado por la edad viril (247).
Of course, since Ganivet maintains that Latin America is basically like Spain, it would appear to follow that Spain, too, must still be in its infancy. But one cannot pause to criticize all Ganivet's inadequacies. The character of Latin American nations, like that of the United States, has been determined principally by succeeding generations of adults. For objections to Ganivet's type of imagery and the manner of thought that it reveals, see, among others, H. Frankfort, *The Birth of Civilization in the Near East*, London 1954, pp. 23–4, and Popper, *The Poverty of Historicism*, pp. 111, 114, 119. I find the following observation by Professor Popper especially relevant to Ganivet:
In many historicist and evolutionist writings it is often impossible to discover where metaphor ends and serious theory begins (op. cit., p. 119).

Conception (the conception of Mary, Mother of Jesus, free from the taint of original sin) with that of the virginity of the Mother of Christ. To Unamuno's objection Ganivet replied, *inter alia*, that someone had pointed this out to him before he published his work but that he had preferred to leave the passage unchanged (II, 1066–7). The confession is revealing and can hardly increase our respect for the author, for by neglecting this pre-publication criticism Ganivet knowingly makes a stronger case than reality in fact allows: in the dogma of the virginity of Mary he finds the exact image of Spain that as a determinist he wants, and in the dogma of the Immaculate Conception he finds the immense popularity that as a determinist he requires in order to present the image as significant. To have proposed the one without the other would have reduced his illustration to its true, rather limited value.

So far we have seen how Ganivet shapes argument (words, concepts, logic, images) to facts. But there is another side to his work: the shaping of facts to argument. There is no need to review here the evidence of earlier chapters: the use and neglect of the 'capítulo de Maquiavelo' that Ganivet found in the incorporation of Navarre into the kingdom of Spain (above, pp. 76–7); the use and neglect of the 'pequeños estados [. . .] encerrados y alejados del campo de la lucha' (above, p. 79); the disregard of the continental or peninsular origin of most of the world's 'aggressors' (above, pp. 82–3) . . . But one must recall, at least, the evidence of other scholars who have probed more critically than I myself have felt competent to do into Ganivet's interpretation of historical facts (above, pp. 89–91). Manuel Azaña's study is the most comprehensive and the most revealing on this aspect of the *Idearium*, and his findings are summed up with admirable brevity in the following words:

Los medios intelectuales de Ganivet son harto inferiores a sus propósitos (*Plumas y palabras*, Madrid 1930, p. 92).

Indeed, Azaña's study alone is sufficient to convince one of the undeniable truth of this claim.[1] But to oppose Ganivet with historical facts is perhaps to take him too seriously. For Ganivet, even though he writes on the problem of Spain, is little concerned with objective historical realities. He is haunted by 'el desprecio del mundo sensible, el asco del espíritu por la materia; hablando en tono materialista, la incapacidad para asimilarse los elementos exteriores' (II, 811). Scholars, he claims, have looked at things too closely and have lost themselves in their analyses. More abstraction is required. But as we saw in the last chapter, Ganivet himself offers little evidence that his own abstractions bear any relationship to historical realities. His concern, I have said, is not to study but to explain and, especially, to justify that 'destello divino' that is born within him when the confused ship of reality is still on the distant horizon, before it approaches port. I recall again the conclusion of the passage referred to:

Por un instante que el alma se deleite en la contemplación de una idea que nace limpia y sin mancha entre las espumas del pensamiento, ¡cuánta angustia después para hacer sensible esa idea en algunas de las menguadas y raquíticas formas de que nuestro escaso poder dispone!, ¡cuánta tristeza al verla

---

[1] Dejando sentimentalismos a un lado, sólo con la lógica rigurosa de la modalidad intelectual que lo distingue y el dominio de una vasta cultura histórica y política, Azaña pone de manifiesto, ora la debilidad, ora la total falsedad de mucho del contenido del ensayo de Ganivet (César Barja, *Libros y autores contemporáneos*, Madrid 1935, pp. 16–17).

convertida en algo material, manchada por la impureza inseparable de lo material! (199–200).

Ideas are born in all their purity and then are tarnished
and deformed by the incursions of reality. It may well be
so. Certainly, many poets have proclaimed it to be so and,
like Ganivet, sought to project their own inner reality
upon the reality around them. But Ganivet is not a poet
and he is not involved in the poet's task. What is admissible in the lyric poetry of an Espronceda or a Pedro
Salinas is not admissible in what purports to be a serious
study of the problem of Spain. The poet is permitted—
more than that, he is required—to re-create reality by
projecting himself upon it. The student of a civilization,
on the other hand, must surely submit himself to the
object of his study. Of course, the field is vast and complex, and the scholar must select and grade his evidence.
Moreover, in that selection and grading it will be extremely
difficult, and perhaps impossible, for him to be completely objective. But objectivity will at least be his aim,
and reality will be greeted by him not as a tarnisher and
corrupter of the purity of his ideas, but firstly as a source
of evidence suggestive of hypotheses, and thereafter as a
source of fresh material with which to test and progres-
sively to modify those initial hypotheses. But this, I
repeat, is not Ganivet's method. His initial evidence is
inadequate; the ideas that he infers from that evidence
will not stand up to the most superficial test of reality;
and non-conformity to his naïve schema, whether it be of
scholars or of historical facts and personages, is simply
dismissed with expressions such as 'tontos' (157), 'ab-
surdos' (182, 226), 'insigne mentecato' (168), 'hipo-
cresía sistemática' (191), 'ceguedad intencionada o volun-

taria' (191), 'refinada estupidez' (231). The *Idearium* is not a work of serious study; it is a work of intoxicated and dogmatic self-justification.[1]

But is this not the case with many a great work of literature? The greatness of a creative writer, I have suggested, will depend not on his function as a mere 'reflector' (278), but, on the contrary, on his ability to re-create reality in terms of his own preoccupations (above, pp. 125-6). The difficulty lies perhaps in the term 'creative', for literary creation as I understand it presupposes two things: a particular, personal vision of reality, and the ability to communicate that vision by means of words. In the former, it seems, Ganivet is clearly a potential creative artist, for he sees reality as a unified and coherent expression of his own personal preoccupations. One may object that the field upon which he seeks to project his preoccupations is inappropriate and, because of his self-projection, one must certainly exclude him from serious consideration as a historian or as a 'psicosociólogo'.[2] But he may yet justify himself as a creative artist. Thus, in a recent study of Azorín's *La ruta de Don Quijote* I have tried to show, as here with Ganivet's *Idearium*, that the underlying thought is determinist, but that, again as in the *Idearium*, the author's determinism breaks down under the impact of personal obsessions. My

[1] Pieter Geyl's criticism of another 'prophet' of civilization is clearly relevant to Ganivet:

He dwells in a world of his own imagining, where the challenges of rationally thinking mortals cannot reach him. Prophets will at most traduce and scoff at their critics. As to showing that their critics are wrong, why should they? They know in their inmost hearts that disagreement can only spring from infidelity (*Debates with Historians*, p. 177).

[2] Ganivet deja un nombre, del más fuerte y subido valor, como 'psicólogo de los pueblos', o psicosociólogo (QS, p. 173).

findings up to this point, then, are basically the same as on the *Idearium*:

> Despite Azorín's declared determinism and despite his clear acceptance of determinist assumptions in *La ruta de Don Quijote*, from a purely determinist point of view the work is unsatisfactory. It is emotion, not intellect, that gives the work its real unity and it is as the communication of a particular, personal view of life that it must ultimately be judged (*La ruta de Don Quijote*, Manchester University Press, 1966, p. 177).

But at this point in one's study of Azorín, one's real task has scarcely begun, for the author's guiding preoccupations are only a framework and one then has to examine, as one would with Antonio Machado, as one would with Juan Ramón Jiménez, the means by which the author's particular vision of reality is communicated to the reader —not on a plane of mere logic, but on a more complex plane that invites also the active participation of the reader's senses and emotions. Thus, one must consider how the here-and-now is made the bearer of the author's temporal preoccupations, how it is enveloped in a characteristically Azorinian atmosphere of nostalgia and yearning, how we are persuaded to make the transition from a world of material objects to a realm of the emotions. Repetition and gradation and climax, the careful choice and placing of words, the musician-like use of silence, invitations to the reader to participate in the author's own actions and reactions—all these things play their part, and by bearing the reader away from a plane of mere logic and commonplace reality they enable him to suspend critical disbelief and to share for a while Azorín's own intensely personal vision of the world around him.

But with Ganivet there is little room for any of this,

once one has examined closely the validity of his ideas and the logic—or lack of logic—with which they are presented to the reader. Ganivet's claim to recognition rests primarily on the ideas he presents; Azorín's rests on the emotional atmosphere that he infuses into his writing. Ganivet is a logician; Azorín is a poet. The following two passages, the first from the *Idearium* and the second from *La ruta de Don Quijote*, will serve to illustrate this difference:

Todas las religiones y en general todas las ideas se han propagado y propagan y propagarán en igual forma: son como piedras que, cayendo en un estanque, producen un círculo de ondulaciones de varia amplitud y de mayor o menor persistencia; el cristianismo cayó desde muy alto, desde el [c]ielo, y por esta razón sus ondulaciones fueron tan amplias y tan duraderas.

Pero lo más admirable en la propagación del cristianismo no es ni su rapidez ni su intensidad; porque ¿qué admiración puede causar que en diversos campos simultáneamente labrados, abonados y sembrados de trigo, nazcan simultáneamente muchas, infinitas matas de trigo? Más admirable y extraño es que, por medio de hábiles injertos, nazcan en unos árboles frutos que son propios de otros árboles y que las savias, mezclándose y confundiéndose, regalen el paladar con nuevos y delicados sabores (156).

Pero, lector, prosigamos nuestro viaje; no nos entristezcamos. Las quiebras de la montaña lejana ya se ven más distintas; el color de las faldas y de las cumbres, de azul claro ha pasado a azul gris. Una avutarda cruza lentamente, pausadamente, sobre nosotros; una bandada de grajos, posada en un bancal, levanta el vuelo y se aleja graznando; la transparencia del aire, extraordinaria, maravillosa, nos deja ver las casitas blancas remotas; el llano continúa monótono, yermo. Y nosotros, tras horas y horas de caminata

M

por este campo, nos sentimos abrumados, anonadados, por la llanura inmutable, por el cielo infinito, transparente, por la lejanía inaccesible. Y ahora es cuando comprendemos cómo Alonso Quijano había de nacer en estas tierras, y cómo su espíritu, sin trabas, libre, había de volar frenético por las regiones del ensueño y de la quimera. ¿De qué manera no sentirnos aquí desligados de todo? ¿De qué manera no sentir que un algo misterioso, que un anhelo que no podemos explicar, que un ansia indefinida, inefable, surge de nuestro espíritu? Esta ansiedad, este anhelo, es la llanura gualda, bermeja, sin una altura, que se extiende bajo un cielo sin nubes, hasta tocar, en la inmensidad remota, con el telón azul de la montaña. Y esta ansia y este anhelo es el silencio profundo, solemne, del campo desierto, solitario. Y es la avutarda que ha cruzado sobre nosotros con aleteos pausados. Y son los montecillos de piedra, perdidos en la estepa, y desde los cuales, irónicos, misteriosos, nos miran los cuclillos . . . (Azorín, *OC* II, 277-8).

In both cases the underlying thought is determinist: Ganivet likens the influence of Christianity to the concentric circles produced by a stone falling from a great height, and thereafter presents its propagation among different peoples at the same psychological moment, in terms of the simultaneous growth of seed sown at the same time in different fields similarly prepared; and Azorín emphasizes the vastness of the Manchegan countryside as an important formative influence on Alonso Quijano, the idealist and the visionary. Moreover, from a strictly realistic and logical standpoint it is probable that neither case is justified: neither Ganivet's comparison of the spread of Christianity to circles in water and seed germination, nor Azorín's emphasis on the landscape of La Mancha as an influence on the character and actions of Alonso Quijano. But the difference is clear. In the passage from *La ruta* mere conceptual logic and commonplace reality matter little; Azorín has created his own superior realm of poetic logic and poetic reality; La Mancha—Azorín's La Mancha—lives in its own right, and the reader is made to feel the vastness and the yearning that Azorín himself has felt. On the other hand, Ganivet's evoked plane serves not to move his reader's affections, but simply to illustrate an argument; at no point does it take on its own particular existence; it remains a mere handmaiden of logic.

Moreover, I have here chosen a passage that contains some of Ganivet's more acceptable images. But now let us consider an image that is rather less acceptable. The author is emphasizing the importance of stoicism in Spain's 'ideal constitution':

> El espíritu español, tosco, informe, al desnudo, no cubre su desnudez primitiva con artificiosa vestimenta; se cubre con la hoja de parra del senequismo; y este traje sudario queda adherido para siempre y se muestra en cuanto se ahonda un poco en la superficie o corteza ideal de nuestra nación (152).

It is a grotesque image and it confuses the case presented: stoicism as a minimal covering (though it has previously been presented as the basis of Spain's 'ideal constitution'), a minimal covering which, a moment later, is an all-embracing dress that sticks permanently and reveals itself whenever one probes beneath the surface (the skin, presumably). Moreover, besides misrepresenting what the author has already said, the image throws up a problem: if *el senequismo* is mere covering, what is the 'desnudez primitiva' that it covers? If this 'desnudez primitiva' is relevant to Ganivet's case, it should surely be explained outside the context of the image; if it is irrelevant, this is yet another weakness of the image.

The case, I believe, is clear and further evidence would simply labour the point. *Idearium español* is characterized by an intensely personal view of Spanish civilization and this view stems ultimately from Ganivet's own tormented mental and emotional state. It is not Spanish civilization studied and documented and abstracted; it is Spanish civilization as 'destello divino', an 'ideal' system born 'limpi[o] y sin mancha entre las espumas' of Ganivet's own imaginings. Consequently, however great the personal therapeutic value of the work may have been to its author, as a study of Spanish civilization it is little more than worthless. Ganivet is not a serious student; he is a potential poet. But in the *Idearium* at least his potential is unrealized. He is singularly insensitive in his use of language and despite his inner world of passions and torments he rarely lifts himself or his reader beyond a plane of mere logical—or illogical—argument. In *Idearium español* Ganivet has sought to rationalize his emotions, and vocabulary, concepts, logic, images and facts are all forced into the narrow mould of a naïve determinist system. Why, then, has the work been considered so highly? We have seen some of the possible reasons, but they alone, I feel, are not enough. I shall look for further reasons in my next and final chapter.

VII

IDEARIUM ESPAÑOL IN ITS AGE AND IN POSTERITY

I must make it quite clear. I have not attempted in the preceding chapters to exhaust criticism of Ganivet's *Idearium español*. I have simply sought to illustrate briefly my main objections to the work. Indeed, an exhaustive—or even nearly exhaustive—criticism would have taken too much time, too much space and, very especially, too much patience. For it is my belief that no page of the *Idearium* can elude adverse criticism entirely. Sometimes it is a matter of factual error, sometimes a matter of illogical reasoning or self-contradiction or an unjustified *deus ex machina* or a misleading comparison or anecdote; sometimes it is a question of over-simplification or of manifestly exaggerated determinism, sometimes a clearly mistaken prediction, sometimes a case of personal or national prejudice or the expression of a value judgement that is irrelevant to the matter under study. But I have not listed examples of such weaknesses at length. I have considered it sufficient to offer brief illustrations of those that I find most significant.

Nevertheless, if the criticisms I have made are justified —or indeed only a substantial part of them—one is forced to ask oneself why *Idearium español* has enjoyed such a high reputation during the seventy years since it first appeared and why Ganivet, principally because of this one work, has been acclaimed as the greatest Spanish thinker since the seventeenth century. Certain reasons have already been suggested: the appeal of the work's simple yet apparently comprehensive intellectual schema; the apparent authority that is given to the work by the use of terminology and concepts derived from the natural sciences; the superficially skilful bending of argument (words, concepts, logic and images) to facts, and of facts to argument. But all this, I feel, is not enough and my aim in this chapter is to look for other, more potent reasons for the *Idearium*'s success.

May the propaganda of enthusiastic friends have been such a reason? Certainly no writer's memory can have been more fervently tended by his friends. His essential goodness and humanity, his modesty, his complete disinterestedness, his prodigious memory, his vast knowledge, his incredible depths of thought, his astounding originality, his remarkable efforts to promote the intellectual and literary regeneration of his native Granada —these points were pressed again and again in the years immediately following Ganivet's death and they have been duly repeated and developed during the succeeding decades. 'Creo que conocía todo lo principal que ha producido el pensamiento humano en el mundo,' wrote Nicolás María López, 'y al exponerlo de palabra, en rapidísimas síntesis, dejaba a uno deslumbrado' (in *Madrid Cómico*, 10 December 1898), and elsewhere: 'No he visto nada tan parecido a la santidad como los arranques generosos del alma de Angel Ganivet' (in *La Alhambra*, 30 November 1898). 'Ganivet fue, para sus amigos de Granada, lo más parecido a un oráculo,' wrote Francisco Seco de Lucena in his Prologue to *El escultor de su alma* (1904, p. 11), and Rafael Gago y Palomo recalled him as the Ulysses of the intellectual Odyssey of raising up Granada and Andalusia, a new Plato, an Aristotle dispensing philosophy in his walks; 'era de la sustancia de que se hacen los apóstoles (in *La Alhambra*, 30 November 1900), the Isaiah of this Jerusalem of Granada, destined perhaps to herald in 'lo que Israel llamó "el periodo de los profetas"' (Prologue to *Granada la bella*, 2nd ed., Granada 1904, pp. xiv–xv). And for Francisco Navarro Ledesma, the most fervently Messianic of all Ganivet's friends, the deceased writer was 'el hombre de inteligencia más elevada y comprensiva, de voluntad más dura para lo bueno, y de corazón más noble y tierno que yo he conocido ni pienso conocer' (in *El Globo*, 5 December 1898), 'un hombre único y señero, distinto y desligado en todo y por todo de los demás seres humanos, un eslabón roto de esta servil cadena que humanidad se llama [. . .], tipo humano o superhumano de transición', exerting 'inexplicable e imperioso influjo, tal como debieron ejercerle todos los precursores y todos los Mesías', dying at thirty-three like Christ and, in his lifetime, understood and loved and followed by women 'con aquel instinto sublime con que otras mujeres de otros tiempos siguieron al Redentor y le acompañaron hasta el pie de la cruz' (*Angel Ganivet*, Valencia 1905, pp. 12, 14, 23, 26–7).

Such enthusiastic—if at times distasteful—panegyrics, together with the tragedy of Ganivet's early death, doubtless played a considerable part in bringing the deceased writer to the attention of the Spanish reading public. But from the propaganda of enthusiastic friends to the esteem of enlightened contemporaries of the stature of Unamuno, Maeztu and Rafael Altamira there is surely some distance, something more than the audacious 'golpe de mano de la crítica' to which Cardenio (Manuel Azaña) was later to attribute Ganivet's reputation as 'inventor de España, apóstol y fundador de la patria espiritual venidera' (in *La*

Pluma, February 1921, p. 89). It is this deeper reason for Ganivet's acceptance as a great writer and outstanding prober into Spanish destinies that we are here concerned with.

The following lines, with which Leopoldo Palacios ended his lengthy review of the *Idearium* in 1898, will serve as a pointer to my case:

> y, francamente, en los momentos de adversidad y de flaqueza, de decaimiento del espíritu que vivió en la gloria, consuela el recuerdo del pasado; y pensando en que llegamos en la evolución a vivir para nosotros, embriagados por la propia vida, dan los efluvios de la patria alientos a la juventud que, con generosas aspiraciones, contempla el ideal y se apresta a la reforma (In *Revista Crítica de Historia y Literatura* III, 1898, 280).

The *Idearium* established itself in the affections of the Spanish reading public at a time of extreme national adversity and it did so, I suggest, principally because of the consolation that readers found in it.

A review of the Spanish press during the years 1896–8 offers evidence enough on the first point. 'De la guerra', 'Terrible catástrofe', 'La insurrección de Cuba', 'La rebelión de Filipinas', 'Corrida a beneficio de los soldados', 'Carreras de velocípedos a beneficio de los soldados', '10.000 hombres más a Filipinas', 'Tropas a Cuba', 'Socorros a los soldados', 'Función a beneficio de los soldados', 'El conflicto con los Estados Unidos'—these are the characteristic headlines of the time. On 1 January 1897 the Madrid periodical *Apuntes* published a long and depressing review of the year that had just ended:

> En Cuba guerra con los negros, con los malos españoles, con el clima y con los Estados Unidos, únicos que sostienen, moral y materialmente, la rebelión. En Filipinas guerra con

los malayos, con los masones y quizá con otros enemigos
que no pasan por tales [. . .].

De todo lo anterior [it concluded] se deduce que nos
haría un señalado servicio la divina Providencia si nos diera
un año 97 un poquito mejor que el 96.

But 1897 was not better than 1896, and 1898 was worse.
On November of this last year the signing of the Paris
peace treaty brought the war to an end and proclaimed
aloud the defeat of Spain as a colonial power. The following lines from *El Liberal* ('el periódico de mayor circula-
ción de España') convey, perhaps, as well as anything, the
national feeling of despair:

Hoy se firmará en París el Tratado por el cual renuncia
España a la posesión de Cuba, de Puerto Rico y de Filipinas.

Hoy se cerrará para siempre la leyenda de oro, abierta por
Cristóbal Colón en 1492, y por Fernando de Magallanes en
1521.

Los tres meses y medio invertidos en estériles nego-
ciaciones diplomáticas habían embotado la sensibilidad del
pueblo español, y héchole perder en parte la noción de su
inmensa desdicha.

Hoy, ante el despojo material, despertará de su sopor,
sentirá el desgarrón en la carne viva, y recobrará, para
maldecir y abominar de los que a tal abismo le han empu-
jado, el uso de la propia conciencia.

No somos ya potencia colonial, ni tenemos nada de lo que
todavía constituye el orgullo y el provecho de las de
segundo y tercer orden.

Holanda, Dinamarca, Portugal, conservan y explotan
vastos territorios en Asia, Africa y Oceanía.

Nosotros lo hemos perdido todo. Apenas si nos quedan
en el golfo de Guinea algunos islotes inhospitalarios y en el
Norte de Marruecos unos palmos de costa y media docena
de peñascos bautizados con el siniestro nombre de presidios.

Al cabo de cuatrocientos años volvemos de las Indias

Occidentales, por nosotros descubiertas, y del extremo Oriente, por nosotros civilizado, como inquilinos a quienes se desahucia, como intrusos a quienes se echa, como pródigos a quienes se incapacita, como perturbadores a quienes se recluye.

Desde hoy no será el símbolo nacional un león colocado como señor entre dos hemisferios.

Lo será uno de esos infelices repatriados que, sin armas, sin sangre, y casi sin vida, regresan de las que fueron nuestras colonias.

En ellos está representada España, consumida por la anemia, rendida por la inanición, más que por la derrota, y tan privada de energías como de recursos [. . .].

('Día nefasto', in *El Liberal*, 28 November 1898)

In the conclusion of this leader, the writer emphasized both the need and the desire to turn away from the failures of the past and to discover new paths:

Día de expiación es el 28 de Noviembre de 1898, pero lo será también de suprema y última despedida a nuestra personalidad, a nuestra independencia y a nuestras esperanzas, si no lo tomamos como punto de partida para emprender vías nuevas, y para enterrar definitivamente los vicios pasados y los sistemas caducos.

Para modificar la función, no hay otro recurso que modificar el órgano; para salvar el tronco que aún vive, no hay otra solución que podar las ramas muertas.

El buque, desarbolado, sin máquina y sin timón, se va a pique.

Echemos al mar la carga inútil, si no queremos que sea completo e irremisible el naufragio.

Two days later *La Vanguardia* of Barcelona made a similar point. After a long period of illness, it declared, our colonial empire has expired, but our grandchildren may yet be grateful for the outcome.

Después de todo ¿por qué no? ... En este momento
tenemos todos la boca llena de una palabra: *Regeneración*. De
dónde ha de venir ésta y por qué medios podremos alcan-
zarla es lo que no sabemos todavía, siendo muy posible que
se pasen aun algunos años antes de averiguarlo. Pero
mucho es ya que tengamos conciencia de que necesitemos
regenerarnos y de que clamemos a gritos por esa regeneración: mucho es ya que después de habernos creído por tanto
tiempo una nación eminentemente guerrera y dotada de
extraordinarias cualidades (aunque sin explotar) hayamos
caído en la cuenta de que todos nuestros históricos lauros
no nos sirven para maldita la cosa (*La Vanguardia*, 30
November 1898).

A sense of despair at the ending of Spain's greatness as a
colonial power and a desire to discover new paths of
national action—these are the two points that occur again
and again in the Spanish press towards the end of November 1898. And in those very days, on 29 November,
Ganivet committed suicide. Within a week his name and
the titles of his principal works were known to every
serious reader of the Spanish press. And some of those
readers, stirred by the enthusiastic obituary praise of
Ganivet's friends, doubtless resolved to read his works
for themselves. And hovering as they were between a
feeling of national failure and a desire for national regeneration, would they not be attracted especially to the
Idearium, that 'especie de filosofía sintética de la historia de
España; un sumario de ideas, un estudio profundo y
originalísimo de la cultura española, de la constitución
ideal de nuestra raza y de los rumbos de la regeneración
nacional'?[1] And would they not be even more attracted

---

[1] Nicolás María López, 'Angel Ganivet', in *Madrid Cómico*, 10 December
1898.

when, on reading the book, they found in it an apparently
logical and coherent exposition of the thesis that Spain's
imperial exploits had been a violation of the nation's
fundamental character (independence) and therefore inevitable, that Spain had been ejected from her colonies
because of her very success in communicating that
character to the colonies,[1] and, again with the authority of
alleged historical necessity, that withdrawal from imperial exploits was the indispensable preliminary to *true*
national greatness?[2] Nor did the consolation end there,
for Ganivet maintained that, being the first to bring to an
end her material evolution (he avoids the word *fracasar*),
Spain was ahead of other nations, at the forefront of
historical evolution, and must therefore initiate 'pro-
cedimientos nuevos, acomodados a hechos nuevos
también en la Historia' (280-1). It is difficult to imagine a
more dexterous plucking of victory from defeat, and
Ganivet's view of Spain's new role, 'iniciadora de pro-
cedimientos nuevos', together with his accompanying
reflection that all nations would inevitably lose their
power one day (ibid.), was to be quoted frequently in the
years following the Disaster.[3] And, of course, there was a

[1] Este carácter que nosotros sabemos infundir en nuestras creaciones
políticas y en el que damos el arma de la rebelión, la fuerza con que
después somos combatidos, es una joya de inapreciable valor en la
vida de las nacionalidades, pero es también un obstáculo grave para el
ejercicio de nuestra influencia (248).

[2] De aquí la necesidad perentoria de destruir las ilusiones nacionales;
y el destruirlas no es obra de desesperados, es obra de noble y legítima
ambición, por la cual comenzamos a fundar nuestro positivo engrandecimiento (271).

[3] nosotros, aunque inferiores en cuanto a la influencia política, somos
superiores, más adelantados, en cuanto al punto en que se halla nuestra
natural evolución; por el hecho de perder sus fuerzas dominadoras —y
todas las naciones han de llegar a perderlas— nuestra nación ha entrado
en una nueva fase de su vida histórica y ha de ver cuál dirección le
está marcada por sus intereses actuales y por sus tradiciones (281).

What commentators overlooked, however, in their enthusiastic references

still greater consolation offered, for though Ganivet recommended withdrawal from material involvements in
Latin America, he did not renounce the idea of Spain's
mission in the New World. On the contrary, he recommended physical withdrawal so that Spain could concentrate her energies, restore her forces, develop her
intellectual and spiritual powers, and make herself
eventually the true leader of Hispanic peoples everywhere.

It is a noble ideal, and after a century of colonial
disintegration, after the horrors of physical involvement
in Cuba and the Philippines, it is understandable, and
indeed perhaps inevitable, that a country educated to its
crusading mission should find in the *Idearium* a balm for
its sufferings and accept gratefully the substitute, however
badly argued, of a spiritual crusade. But from gratitude
for timely consolation, to praise of the *Idearium* as a great
study of Spain's situation in the world was too easy a step
and too few writers resisted it. The *Idearium*, wrote
Francisco Seco de Lucena in 1904, 'es la obra más con-
soladora, y de más noble hermosura, de más sano patriotismo y de más elevada filosofía política que se ha publicado
durante el último siglo en nuestro país'.[1] Is it unfair to see
here a cause-effect relationship between the writer's
gratitude and his enthusiasm? I believe not. And here is

---

to this passage, is that if eventual loss of power is to be the lot of all nations
(including island nations whose aggression is in harmony with their territorial spirit), Ganivet's determinist view of the territorial spirit then
becomes less relevant to his explanation of Spain's own colonial failure.
The very profusion with which Ganivet offers consolation—here the
peninsular inevitability of Spain's failure, plus the dog-in-the-manger
assurance that *all* other nations will follow—does at times undermine his
basic schema.

[1] Prologue to *El escultor de su alma*, Granada 1904, p. 24.

N

another quotation that, for me at least, points to a similar progression from gratitude to admiration:

> La más digna de admiración entre todas las características de Ganivet es su entusiasmo por las cosas de España y su confianza ciega en que las fuerzas nacionales latentes podrán desenvolverse un día en espléndidas manifestaciones que asombren y maravillen al mundo entero (J. Valenzuela La Rosa, in *Revista de Aragón* VI, 1905, Secciones de Filosofía, Pedagogía, etc., p. 45).

We could cavil at the value of 'confianza *ciega*' (the word, alas, is only too well chosen), and regret that critics have too often allowed their own desire for a national mission to blind them to the fundamental inadequacy of Ganivet's case. But in times of illness one takes one's medicine where one can, and it is perhaps significant that Rafael Altamira, one of Ganivet's earliest champions, was also one of the writers of the time most anxious to replace the current pessimism of Spain by optimism and to rejuvenate the country by offering it ideals:

> Pueblo que se considera a sí mismo como degenerado, como inepto, como incapaz de esfuerzos regeneradores [. . .] es pueblo condenado al pesimismo, a la inacción y a muerte segura y rápida. Pueblo que cree en la virtualidad de sus fuerzas, o tiene de su valor presente un concepto elevado (quizá excesivo), se atreverá a todo y sabrá salvar las crisis pasajeras y los tropezones accidentales. Las ideas son fuerza y la engendran (*Psicología del pueblo español*, Madrid and Barcelona 1902, p. 140).[1]

But can this be pushed to the extreme of living a life-lie in the hope that it will one day become reality? Or will the

---

[1] For Altamira's insistence on the importance of a regenerative ideal, see also: op. cit., pp. 141–5; 'El renacimiento ideal de España', in *La Vanguardia*, 22, 24, 26 September 1897; 'Sobre el espíritu de la juventud', in *Boletín de la Institución Libre de Enseñanza*, January 1898.

knowledge that one is living a life-lie eventually seep through and impress with even greater anguish the chasm between image and reality? The questions need not be debated here. It is sufficient to have noted that the evidence that Ganivet adduces in the *Idearium* in support of the consoling ideal of a national mission for Spain does not stand up to the most superficial test of reality or of logic. If Spain's proper role in the world should be to make herself the spiritual leader of Hispanic peoples everywhere, and even, in the words of one commentator, to become 'la única reserva espiritual de Europa',[1] this must be shown with facts and arguments different from those adduced in the *Idearium*. To overlook the inadequacies of Ganivet's case merely out of a desire to accept his conclusions is hardly worthy of the serious reader, much less of the serious commentator. The barometer of the *Idearium*'s success may well be one measure of the Spanish reading public's willingness or unwillingness to face up to political realities.

If this is so, the picture is not a happy one, for in the seventy years that the *Idearium* has been before the Spanish reading public, published objections at least have been remarkably few. The tacit inference of greatness from faith in Spain's mission has been repeated in study after study, the work's extraordinary merit has been proclaimed from decade to decade, and 'detractors' of the work have been reviled as 'los hombres de la Antiespaña', presumably on the unproven assumption that whoever, like Ganivet, proclaims aloud his faith in his country's future must necessarily be a great thinker and a great

[1] Y es Ganivet también quien ve que España puede ser, en el futuro, la única reserva espiritual de Europa (Antonio Gallego Burín, *Angel Ganivet, su españolismo y vigencia*, Tetuán 1951, p. 40).

writer.[1] And here, perhaps, we touch on the key to the pre-Azaña all-party fervour for Ganivet that was illustrated in my first chapter. For about Ganivet's love of Spain, his ideal Spain, and his desire for Spain to gather her squandered energies, raise herself from the ruins of empire and find a worthwhile role in the world of the future—about all this there can be no doubt. Nor, surely, can there be any doubt that, whatever their opponents may say, Socialists, Liberals, Falangists and Carlists here share Ganivet's love and longings. It is in the means by which restoration should be brought about that the real differences appear and in the precise definition of the country's future role, and here Ganivet gives little guidance. He admits losses that are irretrievable (which politician does not?) and presents them as gains (which politician would not like to?). Thereafter, he urges material regeneration (naturally enough) and offers a spiritual crusade capable of appealing to every Spanish heart. It is no wonder that politicians of the most varied opinions have sought to enlist his support and have ransacked his writings for evidence of their own beliefs.

[1] Francisco Elías de T. Spínola, *Ideas políticas de Angel Ganivet*, Madrid 1939, p. 44.
Cf. Para los seguidores del negativismo inerte del mismo año del desastre español, como Ortega y Gasset y Azaña, esencialmente sin comprensión para lo español, en un afán europeizante y universalista que nunca les llegó porque sólo sabían oponer a él, al fin, el pintores-quismo español, con dejes de señorito castizo o pedantes indagaciones, Ganivet sólo merece un frio desdén o un ataque irrazonado e irrazo-nable (Joaquín de Entrambasaguas, 'Angel Ganivet', in *Las mejores novelas contemporáneas*, I, Barcelona 1957, 1160–1).
By 'frío desdén' Entrambasaguas clearly refers to Ortega (see above, p. 31, n. 2), by 'ataque irrazonado e irrazonable' to Azaña (see above, p. 25). The attentive reader of Azaña's article will be amazed that anyone with even a modest use of reason can refer to it as 'irrazonado e irrazon-able' (contrast Barja's opinion, above, p. 167, n. 1). However, in reading 'studies' on Ganivet and his work, one soon learns to be amazed at nothing.

Nor has this been a difficult task, for Ganivet, as we have seen, operates between mutually opposing incentives to action: on the one hand, crusading fervour that calls for expansion without, and on the other, the territorial spirit of independence that demands concentration within. And within this range, critics have taken their stand where they have wished. Recall, for example, Ganivet's treatment of Spain's possible mission in Africa, which aroused such bitter controversy during the 1925 homage (above, pp. 22–4). According to Professor Eduardo Ibarra, Ganivet maintained that Spain should go to Africa not in a military role but in a missionary role, spreading the Catholic faith and preparing the ground for subsequent cultural influence (Lecture of 26 March in the Catholic Casa del Estudiante). 'Claro es que Ganivet no dijo eso jamás en ninguna parte de su obra,' retorted the Socialist daily, *La Libertad* (27 March). 'Indeed he did,' replied the President of the Catholic Students' Association in the Madrid Faculty of Arts, and he quoted supporting evidence.[1] Of course, the editors of *La Libertad* were closer than their opponents to a proper interpretation of Ganivet's basic case, with its insistence on the need for withdrawal from involvements beyond purely national—or at most, Hispanic—frontiers. But absolute negatives are dangerous in references to Ganivet, especially in questions of Spain's international influence, for however much he may urge withdrawal from extra-Hispanic involvements, he rarely closes the door completely on the possibility of

---

[1] ¿Puede darse nada más bello que civilizar salvajes, que conquistar nuevos pueblos a *nuestra Religión* [*should read*: nuestra religión], a nuestras leyes y a nuestro idioma? [260]
Si por acaso hubiera de intervenir, debe de intervenir, sin abandonar sus ideas, con su carácter total de *dominación católica* [*should read:* con su carácter de nación católica] [260].

some future sally, and crusading fervour is always close
at hand to take over as and when circumstances permit.
'If Spain were strong enough . . .', 'When Spain is strong
enough . . .'—one feels that these thoughts are constantly
in his mind, even as the corresponding expressions appear
frequently in his writings. And this is notably so in the
case of Africa, where Ganivet, like his *alter ego* Pío Cid, is
fascinated by the possibilities of conquest and crusade.
Here, for example, is Pío Cid dreaming of African adventures:

> Luego se sentó y se quedó largo tiempo absorto, con los ojos
> fijos en las costas africanas, tras de cuya apenas perceptible
> silueta creía adivinar todo el inmenso continente con sus
> infinitos pueblos y razas; soñó que pasaba volando sobre el
> mar, y reunía gran golpe de gente árabe, con la cual atra-
> vesaba el desierto, y después de larguísima y oscura odisea
> llegaba a un pueblo escondido, donde le acogían con in-
> menso júbilo. Este pueblo se iba después ensanchando, y
> animado por nuevo y noble espíritu atraía a sí a todos los
> demás pueblos africanos, y conseguía por fin libertar a
> Africa del yugo corruptor de Europa (II, 377-8).

And here is Ganivet himself, writing in *El porvenir de
España*:

> Ahora y antes, el único factor efectivo que en Africa existe,
> aparte de los indígenas, es el árabe, porque es el que vive de
> asiento, el que tiene aptitud para aclimatarse y para en-
> tenderse con la raza negra de un modo más natural que el
> que emplean los misioneros, que introducen, según la frase
> de usted, el 'fetichismo seudocristiano'. El árabe habilitado
> y gobernado por un espíritu superior sería un auxiliar eficaz,
> el único para levantar a las razas africanas sin violentar su
> idiosincrasia. Los árabes dispersos por el Africa están
> oscurecidos y anulados en la apariencia por los europeos,

porque estos no saben entenderse con ellos; nosotros sí
sabríamos. Actualmente la empresa es disparatada, pues sin
contar nuestra falta de 'dineros y camisas', el antagonismo
religioso lo echaría todo a perder. Pero ¿quién sabe lo que
dirá el porvenir? (II, 1078).

But would not involvement in Africa be a violation of
Spain's territorial spirit of independence? Ganivet does
not allow mere theory to fetter him—even his own theory:

Si España tuviera fuerzas para trabajar en Africa, yo, que
soy un quídam, me comprometería a inventar media docena
de teorías nuevas para que nos quedáramos legalmente con
cuanto se nos antojara (*El porvenir de España*; II, 1078).[1]

These lines are a good illustration of the Machiavellian
opportunism that informs Ganivet's political thought and
a revealing confession of the facility with which he feels
able to disguise fact with theory.[2] But as has been pointed
out in an earlier chapter (above, pp. 86–7), Ganivet would
have had to change very little in the *Idearium* in order to
urge or justify Spanish involvement in Africa. He would
simply have had to shift the main emphasis from one pole
of his work to the other: from the territorial spirit of independence to the country's historical crusading fervour.

[1] Compare Pío Cid, 'revolviendo en [su] mente toda la historia de la
Humanidad en busca de las triquiñuelas más sencillas y más seguras' to
win people over to his beliefs (I, 426).

[2] Here I find myself quite unable to accept Gallego Burín's view of
Ganivet as 'enemigo de todos los oportunismos y partidario siempre de
las definiciones claras y de las situaciones francas' (*Angel Ganivet, su
españolismo y vigencia*, Tetuán 1951, p. 23). In this respect, one may recall
Ganivet's defence of Machiavelli in the *Idearium* (184). The following lines,
too, are significant:
El patriotismo debería consistir en trabajar calladamente *hasta que*
fuésemos una nación formal y capaz de imponer respeto a los que hoy
por hoy nos paran cuando quieren con un pedazo de papel (cit. AGM,
p. 93; my italics).
Ganivet would surely have appreciated La Fontaine's 'le droit du plus
fort est toujours le meilleur'.

It is this flexibility of his work—and the freedom it offers to critics to shift the emphasis for themselves—that has made it the centre of so much controversy. It is this flexibility also that has assured its continued success in very different political climates. I devote my final pages to a brief justification of this claim.

I have suggested that in the years immediately following its publication *Idearium español* was seized upon as an opiate for national disaster, a means of attributing Spain's loss of empire to historical necessity and of finding, even in the ruins of empire, a pointer to *true* greatness. The *Idearium*, as innumerable writers have pointed out, is the most consoling work of its generation. But if early writers on the *Idearium*, because of the national context of defeat, laid emphasis, as Ganivet himself did, on the potential fruits of withdrawal from involvement abroad, they did not all neglect the gateways of enterprise that Ganivet left ajar and notably that of Africa which, as Ganivet himself says, 'dejo entornada [. . .] pensando en lo por venir' (II, 1077). In the previous pages we have seen an example of the resulting conflict of interpretation, and the countless conflicts between Europeanizers and Traditionalists could offer similar examples from different fields. But it is sufficient, here, to have offered a single example of the conflict before passing to more recent interpretations of the *Idearium* in which the gateways of enterprise left ajar by Ganivet have been kicked so wide open that it is difficult at times to recognize the Ganivet of national withdrawal who was proclaimed so fervently by his contemporaries and near-contemporaries:

> Ganivet proclama nuestro concepto moderno de hispanidad y, contradictor de sus cerrojos, llaves y candados, va a comenzar a abrir escotillas hacia Oriente, en un sueño de

dominio mediterráneo. Hacia el Sur, con el testamento abierto de la Reina Católica; hacia Oeste, cruzando el Océano, sin más bagaje que la común lengua, y hacia el Norte—aquí sí aislacionismo—, afirmando el carácter peninsular y guerrero, no militar, de nuestro pueblo. Esta es la rosa de los vientos del *Idearium* (AGM, in *Arbor* XI, September–December 1948, 481).

Laín Entralgo had touched on the problem in 1940, when he considered the relevance of the *Idearium* to National Syndicalist ideals (above, pp. 27–9). But Laín did not allow his political enthusiasms and his apparent admiration of the *Idearium* to blind him to the essential difference of emphasis. Ganivet, he declared, tells us only what Spain *is* and not what Spain *can be*; his 'nacionalismo casticista', with its humble acceptance of a purely national role, is to be rejected; '*Sólo* hubo místicos españoles cuando España hablaba al mundo su universal lenguaje de hierro y teologías'.

More recent writers have, like Antonio Gallego Morell, found in Ganivet what Laín Entralgo would have liked to find. Ganivet the champion of withdrawal who left ajar, as a consolation to his contemporaries in mourning for lost empire, an occasional gateway for possible future extra-Hispanic involvement, has become Ganivet the herald of a new generation, 'más llena de fe y de certidumbres'.[1] The moment of Spain's international involvement, which Ganivet placed in the future, has now arrived, it is said, or is on the point of arriving. 'Segura de sí misma, se le abre [a España] un horizonte sin límite, un imperio sin fronteras, de contenido espiritual. Ganivet siembra la idea; José Antonio la convierte en acción.'[2]

[1] Gallego Burín, op. cit., p. 29.
[2] Luis Furones Ferrero, in *Seminarios* 6, May–June 1961, p. 93.

Ganivet, then, with his *ideas redondas* converted into *ideas picudas*, is presented as a guide to the men of 18 July 1936, the forger of 'un pensamiento que alertó espíritus muy despiertos; que indicó rutas que siguieron quienes de verdad se desvelaron y desvivieron por amor a España; que atisbó posiciones que hoy son válidas para disparar sobre objectivos que pueden alcanzarse desde ellas'.[1] He is urged upon readers as a man of today and, in so far as his aims have not yet been fulfilled, as a man of tomorrow also.[2]

The shift of emphasis from the pole of national withdrawal to that of crusading fervour is evident. Consider again, for example, the question of Spain's mission in Africa. Castro Villacañas quotes the following passage and italicizes the word that he finds especially significant:

La guerra de Africa es una prueba patente de que la política africana no está apoyada *aún* por intereses vitales de nuestra nación, sino por entusiasmos populares, vagos, indefinidos ([276], in *Arriba*, 18 April 1965).

Again and again, continues the Falangist writer, Ganivet, with his remarkable foresight, emphasizes the need for a greater Spanish role in Africa. Castro Villacañas' inference is clear: the time for greater Spanish involvement has now arrived. Similarly, on the question of Gibraltar, Villacañas emphasizes the words 'Gibraltar es una fuerza para Inglaterra mientras España sea débil; pero si España fuera fuerte, se convertiría en punto flaco y perdería su razón de ser' (237), and comments: 'La fortaleza de España es el camino para la reconquista de Gibraltar'. Again the suggestion is that now Spain is ready: 'Sólo cuando

[1] Demetrio Castro Villacañas, in *Arriba*, 14 March 1965.
[2] Idem, in *Arriba*, 14 February 1965.

España ha encontrado en su paz y en su estabilidad interior la fortaleza precisa ha podido plantearse el caso de Gibraltar en términos que merecen no sólo el respeto, sino la comprensión y la aquiesciencia de casi todos los países civilizados.'[1] How different this Ganivet is from the one who was presented fifty years before in an anonymous letter published in the Madrid weekly, *España*, urging the advantages to Spain of Britain's continued presence on the Rock (30 March 1916)!

And yet the fault of so much difference of opinion is not wholly that of the critics. Ganivet, with his offer of mutually opposing incentives to action, encourages conflict by allowing his readers to take their stand where they will. There is, in the *Idearium*, little real guide to readers; only an incentive to them to indulge their own private and party passions. And in this, Ganivet simply throws open to his readers his own inner conflicts. For, as we have seen, he is a man torn between extremes: between reality and the ideal, between necessity and desire, between fatalism and the will, between withdrawal and expansion, and to express the conflict in terms that are immediately and obviously relevant to the *Idearium*, between stoicism and fervour, between the realistic acceptance of real-life limitations and a passionate longing for crusade. And which is the dominant force in this conflict? In the *Idearium* the main emphasis is very clearly on the plane of limitation and withdrawal. But is one convinced that Ganivet's main emphasis reflects what he really wants for Spain? I believe not, and one can recall, in this respect, that 'considerable element of sour grapes' that was earlier noted in the author's emphasis on stoic withdrawal (above, pp. 144-8). We have found further evidence in

[1] Idem, in *Arriba*, 28 March 1965.

this chapter, and notably in Ganivet's confessed readiness
to invent 'media docena de teorías nuevas' to justify
Spain's occupation of Africa . . . if only she had the
strength. Consequently, the modern, Falangist interpretation of Ganivet's ideas is perhaps not completely unjustified, even though it does manifestly misinterpret
what Ganivet says in the *Idearium*. After all, in that work
there is, potentially at least, something for everyone, and
Castro Villacañas, in shifting the emphasis from the pole
of withdrawal to the pole of crusade has perhaps merely
replaced the case that Ganivet did make by the one that he
would have liked to make—and doubtless would have
made if circumstances had permitted.

But there is no need to examine Castro Villacañas'
findings here, for my own concern has not been to enlist
Ganivet in any political party. My aim has been simply to
understand and explain his thought as it reveals itself in
his most celebrated work, to examine the value of that
work as a probing of the 'problem of Spain' and, finally, to
demonstrate why, despite what I believe to be its rather
limited worth, the book has prompted so much admiration and so much controversy during the seventy years
that have elapsed since its publication. The story, for me,
has been fascinating but, in the last analysis, profoundly
depressing, for the success of the *Idearium* appears to give
weight to Pío Cid's rather cynical view of humanity:

> Contra lo que creen algunos pesimistas, es más difícil
> gobernar a los animales que al hombre, porque los animales
> no se someten más que a la fuerza o a la razón, interpretada
> por su instinto, en tanto que el hombre se contenta con
> algunas mentiras agradables e inocentes, cuya invención
> está al alcance de hombres de mediano entendimiento (I,
> 345).

In the last chapter of *La conquista del reino de Maya* the shade of Hernán Cortés appears to Pío Cid and reviews the attainments of this 'último conquistador español' in the Maya kingdom. 'Los mayas,' he declares, 'eran felices como bestias y tú les has hecho desgraciados como hombres' (I, 650). Though as a devoted student of Spanish civilization it grieves one to make the observation, one can only feel, as one contrasts the doubtful merit of the *Idearium* with its clamorous reception during the last seventy years, that with too many of his countrymen Ganivet has tragically reversed the process.[1] There were truly great Spanish writers in Ganivet's day, and others have appeared in profusion since that time. But, on the basis of his most celebrated work, Ganivet himself cannot be accepted, even marginally, as one of them.

[1] Compare Ganivet's view of his *alter ego:*
Y su único error, que por ser suyo tenía que ser grandísimo, capital, consistía en creer que en España continuaba viviendo entre salvajes, y que podía someter a sus compatriotas a las mismas manipulaciones espirituales que sin duda ensayó, no se sabe si con buen éxito, en el ánima vil de los negros africanos (II, 26).

BIBLIOGRAPHICAL ABBREVIATIONS

(u.o.s.=unless otherwise stated)

AGM: Antonio Gallego Morell, (u.o.s.) *Angel Ganivet, el excéntrico del 98.* Granada 1965.

DG: *El Defensor de Granada.* The Granada daily that published most of Ganivet's periodical contributions.

HLA, I: Hippolyte Taine, *Histoire de la littérature anglaise*, vol. I [1st ed., 1863]. 4th ed., Paris 1877.

LSLP: Luis Seco de Lucena Paredes, *Juicio de Angel Ganivet sobre su obra literaria* (Cartas inéditas). Universidad de Granada, 1962.

MFA: Melchor Fernández Almagro, (u.o.s.) *Vida y obra de Angel Ganivet* [1st ed., 1925]. 2nd ed., Madrid 1952.

MP, 1918: *Angel Ganivet, poeta y periodista* (Bellos trabajos del gran escritor recopilados por primera vez y comentados por Modesto Pérez). Madrid 1918.

MP, 1920: *Angel Ganivet, universitario y cónsul* (Páginas inéditas recopiladas y comentadas por Modesto Pérez). Madrid 1920.

NML: Nicolás María López, (u.o.s.) *La Cofradía del Avellano* (Cartas íntimas de Angel Ganivet). Granada 1936.

QS: Quintiliano Saldaña, (u.o.s.) *Angel Ganivet.* Madrid 1930.